The Really Practical Guide to Primary Technology

THE REALLY PRACTICAL GUIDE TO PRIMARY TECHNOLOGY

Ron Adams and Peter Sellwood

Stanley Thornes (Publishers) Ltd

First published in 1992 by:
Stanley Thornes (Publishers) Ltd
Old Station Drive
Leckhampton
CHELTENHAM GL53 0DN
England

British Library cataloguing in Publication Data
Adams, Ron
The really practical guide to primary technology.
 – (Really practical guides)
I. Title II. Sellwood, Peter III. Series
372.3

ISBN 0 7487 1174 0

Prepared by *specialist publishing service*s tel: 090 857 307
Printed and bound in Great Britain by The Bath Press, Avon

Contents

Chapter 4: A topic bank for design and technology 44

Chapter 5: A guide to components, materials and tools 116

Appendix 132

How to use this book

This book has been written to help you with the vitally important new curriculum area of technology, whether or not you are closely following the demands of the National Curriculum. It will enable you to start on, or develop, technology work whatever your present knowledge or expertise. It concentrates on design and technology which is expressed as profile component 1 Design and Technological Capability in the National Curriculum document, rather than Information Technology (IT), which is a wider cross-curricular issue. You will find , though, that opportunities for IT are presented where they arise naturally in technology work.

The book provides you with the following resources:

- A large and practical ideas bank of topic-based activities for use with infants and juniors at both key stages 1 and 2 (Chapter 4). This is the most substantial part of the book and provides you with a resource of ready-made activities and an 'off-the peg' scheme of work, should you wish to use it in this way. It also provides complete coverage of National Curriculum requirements:
- A concise analysis of the demands of the National Curriculum (Chapter 1)
- Advice on writing schemes of work, progression, recording and assessment (Chapter 2)
- Practical advice and ready-reference guides to organisation and management, tools, materials and components (Chapters 3 and 5).

The book has been written so that you can access material according to your own needs. If you are trying to come to terms with the demands of the National Curriculum you will probably find it useful to start at Chapter 1 and work through. If, however, you are not concerned with National Curriculum or already have technology 'up and running', you will find the topic bank and the information on tools, materials and resources in Chapters 4 and 5 invaluable to develop your work further, and we suggest that you dive straight into these sections.

Acknowledgements

The authors and publishers would like to thank the following:

the controller of Her Majesty's Stationery Office for extracts throughout the book; schools, teachers and pupils throughout England and Wales who have helped directly or indirectly with the production of this book.

Dedication

This book is dedicated to all young technologists in primary schools – including two called Spiros and Socrates.

Introduction

What is design and technology?

When considering how to start this book we looked at a confusing array of statements from official sources for a definition of design and technology. We found that dictionaries define design and technology in a variety of ways.

Design:

- To work out the form or structure..., by making a sketch or plans
- To plan and make (something) artistically or skilfully
- To invent
- To intend, as for a specific purpose, plan
- A plan or preliminary drawing.

Technology:

- The application of practical or mechanical sciences to industry or commerce
- The methods, theory and practices governing such application
- The total knowledge and skills available to any human society.

However, once we started to look at good practice in design and technology within primary schools, much simpler and clearer definitions became apparent.

In terms of the primary classroom and National Curriculum, design and technology may be simply defined as the design process: the cycle of generating ideas, planning, making, evaluating and modifying, which is explained at the start of Chapter 1.

By its nature, design and technology in primary schools has several key features:

It is process-based

Unlike other, more content-based curriculum areas, design and technology is concerned very largely with developing process skills of investigating, planning, making and modifying, and is in this respect very much akin to the investigative skills of science.

It is holistic

Each aspect of the process of design is closely linked to the other parts. In terms of the National Curriculum this means that the attainment targets have to be developed together; they cannot be treated in isolation.

It is cross-curricular

Design and technology continuously draws on and supports work in other subjects, particularly the core subjects of English, maths and science, and has many natural links with the other foundation subjects of history and geography. For this reason it is particularly suitable for cross-curricular topic approaches. This book reflects this fact in the suggestions it makes for delivering design and technology.

It has implications for how you teach

Design and technology demands flexible approaches to teaching and learning. An important feature is that children have to be given opportunities to solve problems for themselves and this puts them, to a certain extent, in charge of their own learning. One aspect of this is certainly allowing scope for group learning, and this in turn may have new implications for the way you organise and teach your class.

Why design and technology matters

Design and technology is important both at school level, for the essential learning skills that it promotes, as well as within the larger social, economic and cultural life of our country. For all cultures at all times the technology of people has given a particular flavour to the age, whether it be the Bronze Age, the age of steam or the nuclear age. Many people today are either excited by the wonderful technological advances of the twentieth century, or horrified by the results of massive failures such as Chernobyl and Kuwait, and the accompanying environmental threats.

However, technology is of fundamental importance to the survival of our culture and to the economic viability and sustainable development of our own country. And yet many people seem to relate design to the superficial enhancement of products almost as an afterthought, whilst many of our best designers and technologists go abroad to develop their careers. It is questionable as to whether the education that our designers and technologists receive reflects the importance of the subject, and there seems little

doubt that at present European children get a significantly better technological education than British children.

It is against this background that the government has introduced Design and Technology as a foundation subject for all pupils aged five to sixteen. As teachers in this newly-defined subject you are faced with a number of challenges and aims. Those aims were clearly expressed in the letter that was sent by Lady Parkes, Chairwoman of the Design and Technology working group, to the Secretaries of State for England and Wales:

> **"** *Our approach to Design and Technology is intended to be challenging and new. The aim of our proposals for Design and Technology is to prepare pupils to meet the needs of the 21st century: to stimulate originality, enterprise, practical capability in designing and making, and the adaptability needed to cope with a rapidly changing society.* **"**

It is almost certain that the SATs for design and technology will be much more prescribed than many had hoped. Do remember that it is essential to provide a stimulating, satisfying and progressive experience of design and technology within a wide and rich curriculum.

Because of the increasing importance of design and technology, our common aim in schools must be to improve design and technology education The immediate task for primary school teachers facing the subject for the first time is to introduce it confidently and in a planned way in individual classrooms as well as across the whole school. This book aims to help this process forward.

1

UNDERSTANDING DESIGN AND TECHNOLOGY IN THE NATIONAL CURRICULUM

The attainment targets and the design process cycle

While it is almost certain that National Curriculum requirements for design and technology will be changed (and that attainment targets may be merged), the main thrust, based as it is on what is commonly known as the *design process cycle*, will remain. The four attainment targets as they are now correspond exactly to the design process cycle illustrated below:

The Design Process Cycle

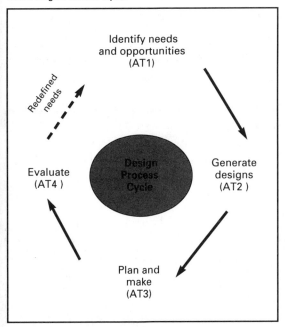

What does the design cycle mean in practice? Here is an everyday example:

Identify needs and opportunities

'Something is eating my strawberries. It seems to be the birds. I need to stop them.'

Generate a design

'My initial idea is to make a cage for the strawberries, covered with a net. I draw a sketch of how I think my cage can be made.'

Plan and make

'I plan the making in detail. I measure. I decide on exact materials (wood, nails, net) and obtain them. I make the cage.'

Evaluate

'The cage looks fine. The strawberries appear to have fewer holes in them. Later I discover a bird has got in under the net. I need to modify the design. I weight the edges to the ground with stones. A week later some strawberries are still getting holed. The slugs are eating them!'

Redefined needs

'I obviously didn't identify my need accurately to begin with. I now have a new need...'

The technology in the National Curriculum document

If you have given even a cursory glance at the *Technology in the National Curriculum* document you will probably realise that it contains a great deal of detailed information, much of which is problematic. The most obvious problem that presents itself is the amazingly complicated relationship between the statements of attainment (SoA) and the programme of study (PoS). This chapter will provide you with a strategy for understanding and relating the two key features in your planning. It concentrates primarily on the design and technology profile components, as information technology (IT) is not really within the scope of this book. However, you will find some mention of IT in this chapter and references to the cross-curricular opportunities for IT in later chapters.

An overview of the document

In common with all other areas of the National Curriculum the attainment targets are specified in terms of 10 levels and there are specific programmes of study for each key stage. The programme of study for design and technology specifies four areas for study. The four areas are:

- Developing and using artefacts, systems and environments
- Working with materials
- Developing and communicating ideas
- Satisfying needs and addressing opportunities.

These are set within widening contexts. The contexts are situations in which design and technology activities take place, including:

- Home
- School
- Recreation
- Community
- Business and industry.

As children develop they will progress from familiar to less familiar contexts.

Furthermore at primary level pupils should develop an awareness of applications of information technology and the ability to use some of these applications in their own work. Design and technology is concerned with process and product and is seen as delivering the three broad areas of knowledge, skills and values.

Technology in the National Curriculum consists of two profile components and five attainment targets as shown opposite.

An overview of the profile components

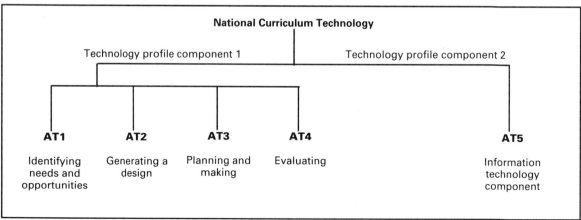

TECHNOLOGY PROFILE COMPONENT 1

Design and technology capability

AT1

Identifying needs and opportunities

Pupils should be able to identify and state clearly needs and opportunities for design and technology activities through investigation of the contexts of home, school, recreation, community, business and industry.

AT2

Generating a design

Pupils should be able to generate a design specification, explore ideas to produce a design proposal and develop it into a realistic, appropriate and achievable design.

AT3

Planning and making

Pupils should be able to make artefacts, systems and environments, preparing and working to a plan and identifying, managing and using appropriate resources, including knowledge and processes.

AT4

Evaluating

Pupils should be able to develop, communicate and act upon an evaluation of the processes, products and effects of their design and technological activities and those of others, including those from other times and cultures.

TECHNOLOGY PROFILE COMPONENT 2

AT 5

Information technology capability

Pupils should be able to use information technology to:

- *Communicate and handle information*
- *Design, develop, explore and evaluate models of real or imaginary situations*
- *Measure and control physical variables and movement.*

They should be able to make informed judgements about the application and importance of information technology, and its effect on the quality of life.

The four attainment targets for design and technology capability are best understood by thinking about them in relation to concrete examples.

AT1 Identifying needs and opportunities

Real needs and opportunities can arise naturally out of the work you are doing with children in the classroom, out of stories that you read with them or out of the immediate environment; for example:

- Postman Pat's bag breaks. Can the children design a better one?
- A lot of litter collects in the playground; it needs to be kept tidier.
- In a historical context, the Roman army are besieging a fortress. They need to batter down the gate. Can the children design a model battering ram?

An important part of identifying a need is research, to pinpoint details of the exact requirement. (In the initial example of the design cycle on page 3, the nature of the need to protect the strawberries was misidentified. Research would have clarified the true nature of the need.)

AT2 Generating a design

Designing is the link between defining a need and making a product. Pupils will need to consider alternatives before deciding what is to be made. From the earliest experiences your pupils will need to communicate their ideas through design proposals. At key stage 1 children will convey their design proposals largely through drawings, models and, most importantly, through talking. Later on, design proposals will be formal and detailed. Such proposals will contain specifications (criteria) against which the finished product can be evaluated.

AT3 Planning and making

This is of course the detailed design and manufacture of the artefact, system or environment. It is important that you do not interpret it too frequently as just making artefacts. The outcome of an untidy classroom might be a system – a rota for litter collection – rather than an artefact such as a bin.

AT4 Evaluating

This should happen continuously throughout design and technology activities, not only after the product has been made. Evaluations might be in the form of fair tests or written reports, or design sketches intended for further modifications. Pupils should be involved in evaluating their own work and that of others, as well as products from other times and cultures.

Generating a design

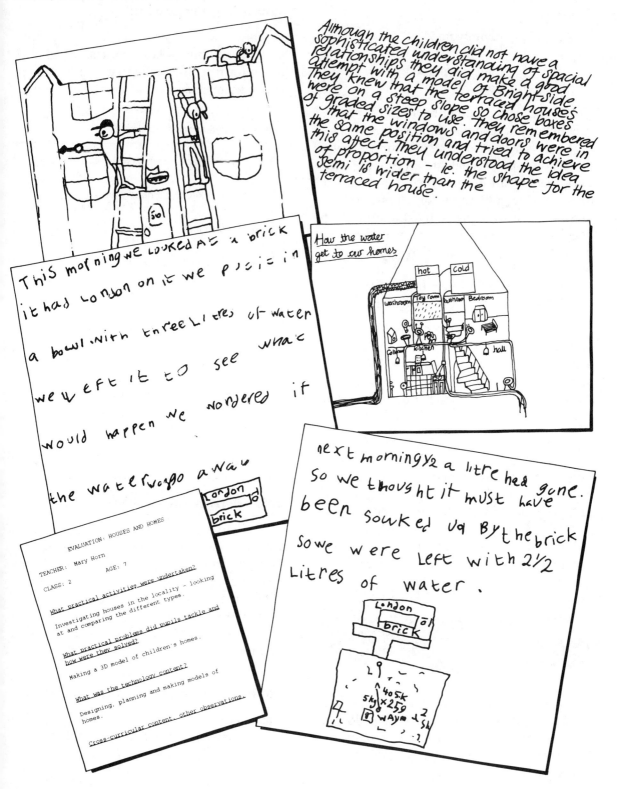

Although the children did not have a sophisticated understanding of spacial relationships they did make a good attempt with a model of Bright-side. They knew that the terraced houses were on a steep slope so chose boxes of graded sizes to use. They remembered that the windows and doors were in the same position and tried to achieve this affect. They understood the idea of proportion - ie. the shape for the semi is wider than the terraced house.

This morning we looked at a brick it had London on it we put it in a bowl with three litres of water we left it to see what would happen we wondered if the water would go away

How the water get to our homes

next morning ½ a litre had gone. So we thought it must have been souked up By the brick So we were left with 2½ litres of water.

London
brick

EVALUATION: HOUSES AND HOMES

TEACHER: Mary Horn

CLASS: 2   AGE: 7

What practical activities were undertaken?

Investigating houses in the locality - looking at and comparing the different types.

What practical problems did pupils tackle and how were they solved?

Making a 3D model of children's homes.

What was the technology content?

Designing, planning and making models of homes.

Cross-curricular content, other observations.

7

Pupils may work in the order of the attainment targets:

Identify needs
Design
Plan and make
Evaluate.

However, this should not be a rigid formula. It is important to understand that *work may start anywhere in the design cycle*; for example, the children might evaluate an existing product, identify the needs which it is intended to meet, suggest ways of improving it, produce their own plans, make the product based on their plans and then evaluate their own product's success. With very young pupils you may start with the making of a product that they find easy to construct and then investigate ways of improving it.

The four attainment targets define activities which are not intended to represent stages in a linear process. They feed both backward and forward into each other, and as pupils work towards one target this will often enhance their achievements in others.

In Chapter 4 you will find a bank of topics that give excellent coverage of all attainment targets at key stage 1 and key stage 2. The topics are headed in each case with a design and technology web that is based on the design cycle on page 3, and you will find that the different topics start at different points on the design cycle.

Understanding the programme of study

The document breaks down the programme of study into four components that do not marry nicely with the ATs. The four numbered components of the programme of study are set out as follows.

PoS1 Developing and using artefacts, systems and environments

Artefacts are objects made by people, systems combine sets of objects or activities to perform a task, while environments are surroundings made or developed by people.

Artefacts, systems and environments

- *a bicycle, bicycle chain, bicycle gears*

- *a house, a kitchen, a hand whisk,*

  model buildings

- *an airport, an aeroplane propeller*

- *a room, curtain, printed fabric*

- *a machine, parts of machines, gears, pulleys*

- *a doctor's surgery*

- *a garden or nature area*

- *a school shop, a supermarket*

- *a castle, a drawbridge*

PoS2 Working with materials

It is important to provide a range of materials that link with the stages of development of your pupils and are part of your strategy for ensuring progression. They will cover the needs of activities that include working with food, fabrics, construction materials and the use of a variety of tools. You will find advice on these aspects in Chapters 3 and 5.

PoS3 Developing and communicating ideas

Imaginative and analytical thinking need to be encouraged and will fuel developments in communication skills.

PoS4 Satisfying needs and addressing opportunities

This is a fundamental requirement that transforms traditional, simple skill-based craft tasks into purposeful design and technology activities.

The programme of study for key stage 1 (levels 1 to 3, ages 5 to 7) is introduced by a general statement:

"Pupils should develop design and technology capability by exploring familiar situations (such as home, school and local shops). They should also look at familiar things (such as pictures, poems, stories, television programmes) as starting points for some of their design and technological activities."

Technology in the National Curriculum (DES, HMSO. 1990)

The programme of study for key stage 2, (levels 2 to 5, ages 7 to 11) is as follows.

"Within the general requirements of design and technology, activities should encourage the appraisal of artefacts, systems and environ-ments made by others as well as the application of enterprise and initiative."

ibid.

There is a distinct difference between PoS and ATs. The programme of study includes specific items that should be taught, whereas the statements of attainment define what your pupils should be able to do or know. For example, the first item in the PoS is at levels 1 to 3, under the heading:

"Developing and using artefacts, systems and environments."

ibid.

It states that pupils should be taught to:

"Know that a system is made of related parts which are combined for a purpose."

ibid.

This, as with other PoS, is accompanied by examples, in this case a bicycle and a house. (The levels are banded to account for the different levels that exist in all classes and the fact that children have different experiences and abilities upon which to build.)

Needs and opportunities in the primary classroom

- *Make traffic lights to control movement along a narrow corridor*

- *Reorganise the home corner in the classroom so that toys can be stored more easily*

- *Identify different ways of making moving teddy bears*

- *Realise that to see how quickly the tadpoles are growing will require a safe way of netting the small creatures*

- *Use knowledge of food and nutrition to try to improve school dinner menus*

- *Find ways of improving the school playground with special attention to safety*

- *Produce an account using maps and graphs of traffic density around the school to support improved provision*

  for cyclists

- *Design and provide a school pets' cemetery*

Relating the programme of study to the attainment targets

The fact that there is no marriage between SoA and PoS is an inexcusable design fault. This disgrace is compounded by the unhelpful way in which the PoS is presented in the document.

Besides the statements in the programme of study that are firmly related to specific levels, the document also contains 34 further requirements that are left floating around in a sea of vagueness. In order to cope with these difficulties, we strongly recommend that you examine the 'floating requirements' and anchor them firmly within your scheme of work. For example the document, under 'Developing and using artefacts, systems and environments' for pupils working towards level 2, states that they should be taught to:

> "*Recognise that control involves making things work as desired.*"
>
> ibid.

This is very similar to the third requirement found under 'Developing and using artefacts, systems and environments':

> "*Give a sequence of instructions to produce a desired result.*"
>
> ibid.

Both requirments can be linked closely to SoA AT1–1b which involves pupils in making suggestions for making games or toys and AT4–2a which involves the ordering of tasks and the efficacy of arrangements.

Should we be working to the attainment targets or programme of study?

You may be unsure whether to follow the programme of study or work to the attainment targets. We are convinced that the best way to deal with this problem is to prepare your own cross-curricular scheme of work into which you have integrated the programme of study for design and technology. Do not work to the attainment targets; you will, however, need to relate these to the programme of study as suggested at the end of this chapter.

We offer an approach to linking statements of attainment and programmes of study that is based on a close analysis of the relationships between them at key stages 1 and 2. We accept that there will be different interpretations of SoA and PoS and recommend our tables as guidelines to a basic plan. You may wish to add to and amend our suggested links between these two vital elements. Although these pages are intended to be a guide only, they provide a strategy for combining the PoS and the ATs. Whether you follow this plan or not, it will be essential for you to relate the SoA and the PoS in order to make sense of technology in the National Curriculum.

Key stage 1 levels 1 to 3 (ages 5 to 7)

Developing and using artefacts, systems and environments

1 Know that a system is made of related parts which are combined for a purpose
AT1–2a

2 Identify the jobs done by parts of a system
AT1–2a

3 Give a sequence of instructions to produce a desired result
AT1–1b; AT4 –2a

4 Recognise and make models of simple structures around them
AT2– 3d

5 Use sources of energy to make things move
AT2–3d

6 Identify what should be done and ways in which work should be organised
AT4–2a

Developing and communicating ideas

12 Use imagination, and their own experience, to generate and explore ideas
AT1–1a, 1b, 2a, 2b & 3b

13 Represent and develop ideas by drawings, models, talking, writing, working with materials
AT2–1a, 3e; AT3–2a

14 Find out, sort, store and present information for use in designing and making
AT1–3a, 4b; AT4–1b

Working with materials

7 Explore and use a variety of materials to design and make things
AT3–1a

8 Recognise that materials are processed in order to change or control their properties
AT4–3b

9 Recognise that many materials are available and have different characteristics which make them appropriate for different tasks
AT2–3b & 3c; AT3–1a & 3d

10 Join materials and components in simple ways
AT3–2b & 3b

11 Use materials and equipment safely
AT3–2c & 3c

Satisfying needs and addressing opportunities

15 Know that goods are bought, sold and advertised
AT1–2c; AT2–3c; AT4–1b, 2b

16 Realise that resources are limited, and that choices must be made
AT1–2C; AT3–3a

17 Evaluate their finished work against the original intention
AT4–2a, 3a & 3b

11

Developing and using artefacts, systems and environments

18 Organise and plan their work carefully, introducing new ideas, so that their work improves
   AT3–5a

19 Allocate time and other resources effectively throughout the activity
   AT2–4c, 5d

20 Control the use of energy to meet design needs
   AT2–5d

21 Use a variety of energy devices
   AT3–3b

22 Plan how practical activities may be organised
   AT2–2a, 4d & 5e

23 Use a variety of information sources in developing their proposals
   AT1–4a, 5a; AT4–3a

24 Use knowledge and judgements to make decisions in the light of priorities or constraints
   AT1–5b; AT2–5b, 5d

25 Identify the parts of a system and their functions, and use this knowledge to inform their designing and making activities
   AT1–4a; AT2–3b, 3d

Working with materials

26 Use equipment safely
   AT3–4c, 5c

27 Select materials for their task
   AT2–5b

28 Rearrange materials to change their strength or character, and increase their usefulness
   AT2–5b, 5d; AT3–4d

29 Join materials in semi-permanent forms
   AT3–2b

30 Assemble materials
   AT3–2b

31 Avoid wastage of materials
   AT3–4a

32 Take responsibility for safe working
   AT3–3c

33 Develop co-ordination and control in using equipment
   AT3–4c

34 Finish work carefully
   AT3–4a

Developing and communicating ideas

35 Take account of other people's reactions to aesthetic characteristics
AT1–4c; AT2–3C; AT4–3a

36 Make the connections between aesthetic characteristics of natural and manufactured objects and relate these to their own work
AT4–2b

37 Plan and structure their communication of ideas and proposals
AT2–2a, 3a; AT3–2a

38 Use drawings and plans to investigate and develop ideas for three-dimensional objects
AT2–3d; AT3–4e

39 Use a range of graphic techniques and processes
AT3–1a, 2c

40 Use modelling to explore design and technological ideas
AT2–3d, 4b

41 Use modelling and recording when generating ideas
AT2–3d, 4a

42 Break design tasks into sub-tasks and focus on each in turn as a way of developing ideas
AT2–3b, 5a, 5b

43 Use materials and equipment to produce results which are aesthetically pleasing
AT3–3c, 4a, 4c

Satisfying needs and addressing opportunities

44 Know that the needs and preferences of consumers influence the design and production of goods and services
AT1–4b, 4c; AT4–3a

45 Recognise the importance of consumer choice and hence the importance of product quality and cost
AT1–4b, c, d

46 Be aware that the appearance of artefacts and environments is important to consumers and users
AT1–4c; AT4–3a

47 Know that human shape, scale, proportion and movement affect the forms of designs
AT4–4d

48 Understand that goods may be designed to be produced singly or in quantity, and that this affects what each item costs
AT4–5a

49 Consider the possible consequences of their design proposals before taking them forward to completion
AT1–5b; AT4–5a

50 Consider the needs and values of individuals and of groups, from a variety of backgrounds and cultures
AT1–4f; AT2–3c; AT4–3a, 4c, 5c

51 Evaluate each stage of their work
AT1–4e; AT2–3e; AT4–3b, 4a, 4b, 5b

52 Make adjustments as a result of evaluation
AT2–3d; AT4–5b

53 Use their appraisal of the work of others to help their own work
AT4–4c, 5c

2

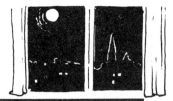

PREPARING A SCHEME OF WORK

In this chapter we consider the construction of a scheme of work and some ways of ensuring progression and development of educational experiences for your pupils in design and technology activities. We also make some proposals for dealing with recording and assessment.

Schemes of work – where to start

We recommend that you start with the programme of study, as it provides a basis of what should be taught during each key stage. When you study the document you will see that you have considerable flexibility over the amount of time to be spent on technology, and that you are not limited to any particular teaching styles or themes, topics, activities or order of activities.

It is useful to read the short examples of the kind of activities that are given accompanying the order, such as:

> " *Prepare a shopping list in order of shops to be visited.* "
> *Technology in the National Curriculum* (DES, HMSO. 1990)

These examples do not always lead to a complete cycle of the design process.

Your scheme of work should be a written statement that will describe the work that you plan for your pupils. Such a plan will normally cover a period of a year or so. The scheme of work should form part of your school's policy; it should include the contexts, concepts and skills to be covered and introduced (and how they are to be introduced) as well as details of the materials to be used. Naturally, you will build such a scheme upon your children's previous experience. In the diagram below we set out how your scheme of work can fit in with other organisational elements in your school's management systems.

Steps in planning a scheme of work

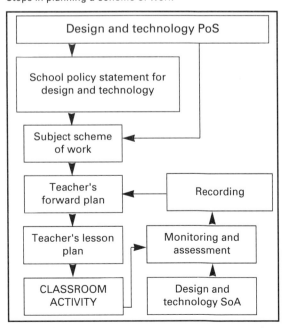

In preparing your scheme of work you may use a combination of two approaches.

Beginning with specific design and technology activities you can analyse which SoA and elements of PoS are covered. Such activities must be carefully selected and matched to ensure that there is an even and balanced coverage of all aspects of the PoS.

The second approach is to work from the PoS and link elements to make complete activities. This approach makes it easy for you to cover the PoS but could be restrictive of your pupils' opportunities to develop tasks in ways that might seem appropriate outside the prescribed areas.

Your tasks should usually include work on all four attainment targets – but not necessarily in the order AT1, AT2, AT3 and then AT4. For example, your pupils may start work by evaluating (AT4) an existing product or may be given a 'set problem' in which the identification of a need (AT1) will not even arise.

Your pupils should be able to decide on the best way of meeting a need or opportunity, although of course you are an essential facilitator of this. At key stage 1 pupils will engage in structured play. At key stage 2 you will help them to their 'discoveries' through careful guidance and assistance. You may find it useful to rearrange the programme of study to help your planning.

Grouping by attainment target

AT1 Identifying needs and opportunities

- Business and economic influences
- Communicating ideas
- Environmental and social influences
- Finding information

AT2 Generating a design

- Material characteristics
- Visualising and modelling
- Knowledge of tools, materials, equipment
- Knowledge of techniques, aesthetic considerations, business and economic methods

AT3 Planning and making

- Organising and making
- Safety
- Skill in using materials
- Skill in using equipment

AT4 Evaluating

- Setting criteria
- Judging against criteria
- Reviewing
- Considering consequences

Safety is an essential part of a scheme of work

Our view is that primary school teachers are best advised to work using their well-established topic approaches. You will find the cross-curricular style will allow you to integrate easily elements from your scheme of work for design and technology into your topics. It will be necessary to include short or 'mini-topics' from time to time to develop knowledge or skill in particular areas such as the safe use of tools, but these activities alone will not develop technology capability.

Your scheme of work should also include regular and appropriate training in safety. Here, of course, a didactic style of teaching is entirely appropriate. Your pupils should be taught to take care of themselves and the safety of others; they should keep work areas tidy and clean. Your school policy document should contain a code of discipline that should be adhered to strictly.

Ensuring progression

If you make use of the programme of study you will almost certainly build progression into your scheme of work. You will satisfy the National Curriculum requirement that:

> " As pupils progress, they should be given more opportunities to identify their own tasks for activity, and should use their knowledge and skills to make products which are more complex, or satisfying more demanding needs."
>
> Technology in the National Curriculum (DES, HMSO. 1990)

How well you satisfy such requirements depends in large measure on the way you differentiate the elements of the problems of progression. Progression includes:

- Increases in skills, concepts (knowledge) and values
- Moving from familiar contexts to unfamiliar ones

- Products that are more complex or difficult to make.

When you are attempting to build progression into your scheme of work, the first step is to ask questions about the present situation in your school:

- Is there well-considered progression already?
- Do children experience increasingly demanding techniques, materials and tools and increasingly demanding contexts in which to employ their developing capability?

A good way to tackle progression is to reintegrate into your cross-curricular programme of study the differentiated elements of progression.

We see those elements as:

- Contexts
- Concepts (knowledge)
- Materials
- Skills.

Progression of contexts

Context is specifically referred to in the National Curriculum document as situations in which design and technological activity takes place and:

> " should include the home, school, recreation, community, business and industry, beginning with those which are most familiar to pupils, and progressing to contexts which are less familiar."
>
> ibid.

The basic idea behind progression is quite simple to understand. Reception class pupils will have their understanding of concepts developed in contexts that are familiar to them; for example the home and school. As children grow, so will the range of contexts in which those concepts will develop. Your pupils' experience will extend out into the environment that is local to the school. Later they may make visits to more distant geographic sites and the calls upon their imagination will be more profound. Eventually pupils will have the context of their educational experiences further extended to include less familiar ones such as businesses and other cultures.

It is essential to examine at the planning stage the potential of topic webs to locate your work in the appropriate context, and to address vital educational areas rather than allow side issues or other disconnected aspects to take over.

Progression of concepts and skills

As pupils grow, so will their skills and the range of materials that are available to them for design and technology activities. Planning for progression can be made easier by identifying a skill and tracking it through the programmes of study; for example:

Programme of study: joining materials

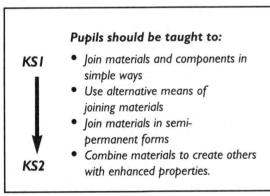

KS1

Pupils should be taught to:

- Join materials and components in simple ways
- Use alternative means of joining materials
- Join materials in semi-permanent forms
- Combine materials to create others with enhanced properties.

KS2

Concepts for very young children that were at first very simple notions, such as heat, will develop with a growing accumulation of classes and sub-classes such as:

- Temperature
- Material (changed by the effect of heat)
- Friction.

The National Curriculum requires that at each key stage pupils should design and make, in response to needs and opportunities identified by them, in the following areas:

- Artefacts (objects made by people)
- Systems (sets of objects or activities which together perform a task)
- Environments (surroundings made, or developed, by people).

Another way of helping to ensure progression of practical activities, in a way that satisfies such requirements, is to analyse the kinds of concepts that should be developed. The type of analysis that you may find useful is exemplified below.

A concept such as 'Structures' may be separated into different classes of structure:

- Supporting structures – towers, pillars
- Bridging structures – beams, arches, suspended
- Housing structures – natural, organic, constructed
- Protecting structures – helmets, packages, clothes.

Progression can be built into your scheme of work since you can increase the difficulty by reference to the programme of study:

Programme of study: structures

KS1

Pupils should be taught to:

- Recognise and make models of simple structures around them
- Recognise pattern in the structures of objects
- Make two- or three-dimensional models of their design ideas and test these further before proceeding
- Recognise and represent organisational structures
- Use knowledge and understanding of materials to design and make structures which stand up to stress.

KS2

Other concepts to be considered include colour, shape, form, texture and energy, control and communication.

Progression of materials

In Chapter 5 you will find a ready-reference guide to the ways materials, components and tools need to be introduced according to a carefully controlled progressive plan. While this chapter concentrates more on concepts and practical skills than on materials, it is worth pointing out that one of the main deficiencies that we have found in schools is that instead of a widening range of materials being made available as children progress from reception classes up through infant and junior schools, the opposite often happens. Consider, for example, the position of water as a material. In reception classes water play is very common. Often, however, by the time children are eight or nine the use of water in class has almost disappeared.

Progression in action: a topic example

This chapter is designed to give you practical help to overcome the problems of progression. It is not possible for us to give you a recipe to ensure progression. What we do offer are examples based upon classroom practice that show how contexts, concepts, materials and skills can be progressed and developed from reception level to top junior. This can be demonstrated by looking at the development which might occur in the same cross-curricular topic from key stage 1 to key stage 2. You will find that the topics in the topic bank show progression across key stages. Here we have chosen the topic of bridges to illustrate how progression actually works in the classroom. The example that we use here is one of the most common topics from within the man-made world and one

A progression in bridge building

LOG ACROSS STREAM

HUMP STONE BRIDGE

SUSPENSION BRIDGE

that is easily associated with design and technology activities. We examine the way contexts, concepts, skills and the use of materials can be developed by revisiting the same topic with the same group of children later in their development. This topic was used with six- and ten-year-olds.

As we present this account we highlight concepts, contexts, materials and skills as they re-occur at the different levels.

Design and technology

*Make bridges using various materials:
bricks, Lego, Multilink newspapers, boxes,
Waffle Bricks, etc.
Make more specific models,with above
materials, e.g. viaduct, suspension bridges
Build strong supports: cubes, bricks, boxes,
side-supports and centre supports and arches
Attempt to make drawbridges
Think about and talk about the best designs*

Language

*Write up experiments
Re-write stories about bridges, e.g. The Cow Fell
in the Canal and Three Billy Goats Gruff
Write-up visits
Make list of new words
Use stories as starting points – Pooh Bridge*

Bridges

Mathematics

*How many cubes can the different bridges
support?
Gather information about the different num-
ber of cubes that bridges can support
Are they strong enough to hold up different
cars? Make a graph of this information
Dice games
Set problems throughout*

Art and design

*Draw children's bridges and famous
bridges
Draw diagrams and label
Make bridge mobiles
Make map of Pooh Bridge*

Religious education

*'Bridges' that bring people together – multi-cultural
Building bridges that can help overcome disabilities*

Bridges key stage 1

At key stage 1 this topic provides plenty of opportunities for making bridges using a variety of materials. Sometimes specific problem-solving targets are involved, such as making a bridge to hold or support a car, or to open and close, or to include an arched or suspension system. If we examine in detail the opportunities for developing concepts and skills and the use of materials we find that the topic is particularly helpful.

Context As required by the National Curriculum, pupils are to develop design and technology capability beginning with things around them such as stories, poems, television programmes, pictures, the school and the home.

Concepts The key concepts listed below are covered:

Assembling

The concept of assembling will be enhanced through fitting things together, junk modelling and using construction kits; strengthening card by folding and gluing pieces together and by using Sellotape and scissors.

Building

Young children will be involved in measuring to make bridges symmetrical; changing size by adding and subtracting and by appreciating that different shapes have different strengths and can meet specific requirements.

Capacity

The concept of capacity will be developed through knowing that large structures will need more bricks in their construction; appreciating concepts such as inside and outside, collating information about the various bridges made and making graphs of the amount of materials used.

Control

Children will have experience of control as they make things go where they want them to go by pushing, putting and pulling, guiding over bridges and down slopes and roads.

Energy

The opportunities for making bridges with moving parts will bring some understanding of the fact that energy is needed to move things including ourselves, toys and models. This can be linked with understanding of the way energy is needed for growth and movement in plants and animals.

Fair testing

A simple understanding of testing will be gained through making bridges that are strong enough to carry a model car.

Materials

The range of materials will include those which are soft, hard, bendy, rigid and floppy. The activities will help your pupils to select the right materials for the various structures that are made with kits, malleable materials and found or 'junk' materials.

Movement

The concept of movement will be shown through pushing, pulling, dropping, rolling and sliding activities.

Shape

Children will use and recognise squares, rectangles, circles, triangles, cubes and rectangular boxes. They will start to understand families of shapes and begin to use them for construction activities as well as for making graphs.

Size

Comparative measuring and, to a lesser extent, accurate measuring will be used. The main considerations will be 'Which is the longer, taller or wider?' Your pupils will also start to use and make measurement units, and similarly will start to develop a comparative understanding of weight.

Solidity

Pupils will start to gain understanding of how some shapes are solid, or rigid, while others are loose or flexible.

Stability

Through exercises such as making bridges with supports and ramps that will span a certain gap, your pupils will have gained experience of developing stability in a standing object.

Structure

Children will understand that buildings and models (and natural objects) have structure.

The practical skills that will be developed include those of assembling, bending, comparing, constructing, cutting, fixing, forming, joining, measuring, modelling, problem-solving, shaping, sorting, testing and tying, including simple stitching.

Language

There will also be many opportunities for improving and extending children's vocabularies. Group discussions following activities involving working in pairs will provide opportunities for pupils to be involved in the evaluation of their own, and others', work. Children will be able to write up reports of their activities.

Common additions to their vocabulary will include, amongst others, such words as: bend, glue, join, make, stand, tall, taller, short, shorter, high, higher, across, over, big, square, rectangle, cube, drive, ramp, roll, slide and support.

Bridges key stage 2

At key stage 2 this revisit to the topic of bridges is based on a historical starting point, a study of early and Victorian bridges with a particular emphasis on the work of Brunel. From this historical origin a problem can be set that requires pupils to:

- Research into the different types of bridges
- Make designs and plans for bridges to satisfy the specified need of spanning a gap of 1 metre
- Select materials from the restricted range provided
- Measure and construct a scale model to satisfy the need
- Evaluate and record the various stages involved in the designing and making processes
- Review their work with the class
- Refine and modify their scale models in the light of the review and evaluation process
- Write up the problem-solving activity.

Although the activities are in some senses more prescriptive than those at key stage 1, development and progression can be seen in the following areas.

Context The stimulus to this type of project at this level can be very much enhanced by visiting sites of different bridges (either famous ones or local, less-celebrated structures). Such visits will extend pupils' technology capability by moving beyond things around them, such as pictures and stories, into a wider context. (In one of the cases that we have seen, the stimulus was given by a visit to the Clifton Suspension Bridge in Bristol.) Discussion about aesthetics, technologies of different cultures (ancient and contemporary) and the way such massive structures can be anchored to the earth's surface will be a useful background to practical activities.

Concepts If you now consider the ways that concepts can be developed you will find that the topic can cover the points listed below.

Assembling

Here pupils will understand that a solid can be made from a number of parts that have been formed separately. Making structures with an extended range of materials that include wood, wire and nylon thread, and making models that have articulated joints that move and have direction, will further extend the understanding of the children.

Building

Pupils will have to understand scale and be able to make models to scale, working from their own two-dimensional designs to make up three-dimensional models. They will build supporting structures, and understand that structures can have moving parts. This can be linked to an understanding that natural structures, such as the surrounding landscape of bridges, can be used as protection, support or as an aid to construction.

Capacity

Pupils will have their knowledge reinforced that large structures require a larger quantity of materials, but the concept of capacity will not be particularly extended beyond the work at key stage 1. You will need to make provision to fill this gap by providing other activities that show that capacity is not only about how *many* but also about how *much*. This is true of solids, liquids, powders, electricity and the information that containers, structures and systems can contain. By doing this you can help form an understanding of the differences between volume and capacity.

Bridges at key stage 2

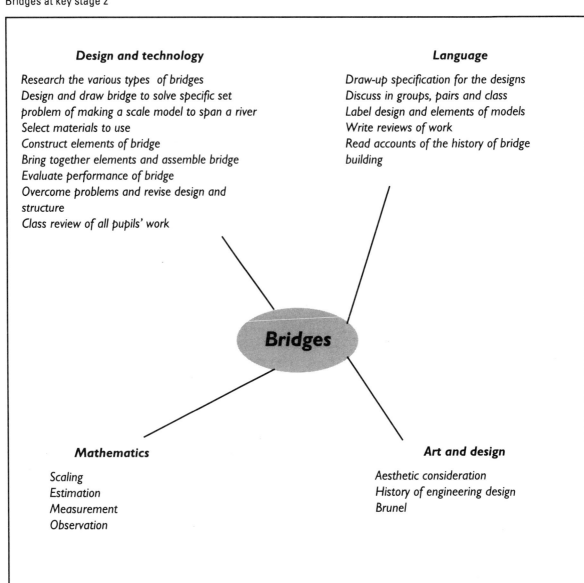

Design and technology

Research the various types of bridges
Design and draw bridge to solve specific set
problem of making a scale model to span a river
Select materials to use
Construct elements of bridge
Bring together elements and assemble bridge
Evaluate performance of bridge
Overcome problems and revise design and
structure
Class review of all pupils' work

Language

Draw-up specification for the designs
Discuss in groups, pairs and class
Label design and elements of models
Write reviews of work
Read accounts of the history of bridge
building

Bridges

Mathematics

Scaling
Estimation
Measurement
Observation

Art and design

Aesthetic consideration
History of engineering design
Brunel

Control

You can ensure that the concept of control is developed by including specific requirements in the problem that you set. For example you can ask that pupils devise a way of controlling the flow of traffic over a single-lane bridge – such as Brunel's. Such a requirement may lead your children to use lighting, switching and computer control.

Energy

If children use lighting, switching and computers they will have the opportunity to understand that energy can be stored in the form of batteries.

You would need to make provision beyond this topic for your pupils to understand that energy can also be stored in springs, elastic and heat; and that energy may be found and used in gravity, water flow, wind and the sun. Also introduce the concept that food is an energy source for all living things.

Fair testing

Because of the differentiation of the components used in the construction of the bridges, pupils will develop their understanding of fair testing. Each individual part as well as the whole structure can be subjected to testing procedures, thereby enhancing the value of fair testing to meet an appropriate variety of needs.

Materials

By building work into a topic plan that involves electricity, it is possible to introduce the concepts of conductivity and flexibility. While a certain extension to the range of materials will be achieved there will have to be much greater provision for this concept in other topics. You need to provide experiences of materials that demonstrate malleability, brittleness, hardness, porosity and buoyancy.

Movement

Pupils will understand the need for transport and movement of things from place to place and that there are different types of transport on land, air, water and in space.

Shape

Pupils will be able to transfer ideas from two dimensions to three dimensions. The links between shape, form and structure will begin to develop.

Size

Accurate measuring and careful scaling up and down will indicate how children's concept of size has progressed.

Solidity and stability

Those pupils who make suspension bridges will develop a particular understanding of how both rigid and flexible materials can be used to produce stable structures. They will understand that joining and fixing can take many forms: rigid, flexible and moving.

Structure

Previous work will be reinforced and children will see that the strength of a structure is dependent on its shape, the way it is made and the materials that are used. They will have opportunities to examine the forces and stresses that are inherent in a structure. Furthermore they will be able to see the importance of design to the function of a structure; that its appearance and stability are linked.

Communication

By the use of designs and written and verbal reviews, children will start to develop an understanding that there are many forms of communicating information – sound, vision, taste, touch and smell – and that information can be stored, relayed and otherwise communicated in various ways.

Language

Children's vocabulary will be extended considerably by revisiting the Bridges topic. Technological literacy is fostered when children's language is developed alongside practical activity. Children will, when encouraged to experiment with words and descriptions, gain confidence and understanding.

There is an increasing recognition that purposeful talk in the classroom assists learning. The role of speech in the learning process is enhanced when children are encouraged to tackle real purposes for talk, a critical issue in raising the status of talk in the classroom. Children's language is greatly extended and enriched by a creative and questioning approach:

" *When young children are involved in some activity, the talk that accompanies it becomes an important instrument for learning.***"**
Bullock Report *A Language for Life* (HMSO. 1975)

The practical skills developed will include those of assembly in which the pupils are capable of making constructions to scale and are able to give buildings texture, colour and a degree of realism. The skills of cutting, bending and forming, including the ability to use a range of tools safely, to bend and form materials with a degree of accuracy and to bore into a range of easily-worked materials, will be extended. The skill of control is exercised when pupils use materials and forces to make structures stand in a stable position and support loads. A different form of control is used over energy sources to operate systems of signalling and lighting. Furthermore, the construction of fair testing is part of the developing skill of problem-solving in children visiting design and technology at key stages 1 and 2.

Ensuring equal opportunities

It is important when producing schemes of work to consider disability, gender issues and cultural diversity.

Disability

The design and technology working group wanted maximum participation in design and technology attainment targets and programmes of study by all pupils, including those with special educational needs.

Those unable to take part in practical activities because of a disability can undertake a closely matching, alternative activity. Children unable to cut material with scissors may be able to separate plasticine or clay into suitable pieces. You will be able to arrange activities that include the use of wordprocessor or graphics packages for those unable to communicate verbally, and thus enable your pupils to satisfy statements of attainment that require them to ask or discuss.

Gender

It is essential to make equal provision for boys and girls to use wood, metal, constructional materials, food and textiles. Boys and girls should be encouraged equally to broaden their experience. Notwithstanding the constraints of staff availability, we believe that you should try to:

- Arrange that pupils see both female and male teachers working with mechanical and constructional material and with food and textiles
- Ensure that pupils see that men and women are not always tied to stereotyped gender-related occupations
- Be aware that pupils' requirements of technology may differ. Boys may be more

likely to think of a career in technology while girls may tend to think of technology as a way of understanding the world – boys and girls do not necessarily work well together.

Cultural diversity

The rich diversity of cultures that we have as a feature of British life can bring great benefits to work in design and technology. You will of course have to take care that some technological language is explained to pupils whose mother tongue has no equivalent for such terms and words. Also you will have to take care about beliefs and practices that involve food and environmental design.

A real opportunity exists for you to show that no one culture has a monopoly of achievements in design and technology. As we nurture our future generations such appreciations can only help contribute to better international understanding and also yield direct economic benefits to the pupils in later life.

Recording

As part of your scheme of work it is essential to make appropriate arrangements for recording and assessment. Records provide evidence for assessment and record the assessments themselves, but keeping them is not an easy task. You must be selective and methodical and remember to collect material that will be easy to access and assess.

Why keep records?

Schools are now under a legal obligation to maintain records of each pupil's progress. For the records of progress in design and technology activities you are required to make a progressive and well-organised record so that teacher assessment (TA), and eventually standard assessment tasks (SATs), can be undertaken.

There are four main functions of records as aids to the processes of education. These functions are:

- Formative
- Summative
- Evaluative
- Informative.

Records contain the evidence upon which assessments can be made.

What to record?

You will need to record pupil progress for each class, or group of pupils. Records will need to indicate:

- Topics/themes covered (including the contexts for design and technology activity)
- Design and technology products.

Individual records of each pupil's experience will be needed. Furthermore your records should:

- Record the attainment targets and statements of attainment which each pupil has attempted
- Show the achievement level which each pupil has reached
- Give an indication of the progress of each individual pupil in relation to attainment targets and statements of attainment
- Be a formative database for individual pupils
- Provide evidence to support the levels of attainment reached
- Give parents and other teachers and schools access to information about their children's academic achievement, other skills and abilities, and progress in school.

The range of material that you need to record

Records can be compiled from:

- Topic (web) forecasts by teachers
- Evaluation of topics by teachers
- Evaluation of specific activities by teachers
- Assessment of pupil performance by teachers
- Self-assessment of performance by pupils
- First-hand evidence of pupils' work.

First-hand evidence could comprise:

- Drawings, designs
- Photographs
- Written descriptions
- Audio and video tape recordings
- Paintings
- Models.

How to keep records

There is widespread confusion amongst schools over what is required of them for the recording of the all-important practical activities. When it comes to guidance to you on what and how to record, SEAC specifically requires you to:

" *Decide what to record.* "

and,

" *Use your usual recording system.* "
A Guide to Teacher Assessment, Pack A
Teacher Assessment in the Classroom
(SEAC. 1990)

The non-statutory guidelines for technology on the management of record-keeping stress the need for record-keeping to be efficient.

This is particularly necessary for technology because of its practical aspects and the

Only collect what is necessary for your pupils' education

variety of activities covered. It is recommended that records should:

- Be simple to complete
- Include all relevant information
- Be meaningful to others who wish to have access to them
- Be accessible to pupils.

It is essential that you are selective in what you keep of work produced by children. All that is kept should be dated, named and annotated at the time it is produced.

Because of the practical aspects of design and technology it is essential to plan recording activities in a firmly structured way. You will need to use the information you gather for a number of purposes and for a variety of audiences. If you look upon the 'raw' information of pupils' work as a pool then you will need to make sure that you have ready access to specific information from that pool.

In order to ensure some degree of consistency between different classrooms a well managed recording system is necessary for you and your colleagues, so that children will not have a fragmented educational experience as they move within the school. Records that are prepared within the terms of reference of the documents that some LEAs are producing will also be very valuable when pupils move to different schools.

Records are kept as a necessary part of planning, organising and monitoring the content of cross-curricular schemes of work. It is recommended that you consider carefully how you are going to undertake the tasks of recording schemes of work and the work of individual pupils.

Try to use the way you work at present as the starting point of a comprehensive and structured system. If you use topic webs and forecasts, keep copies of your topic webs filed in date sequence with the other recorded information. If you note the various SoA and ATs on the web, you will have an easier job when you come to the point of evaluating the topic.

If you write retrospective evaluative accounts try to keep them brief or put them into tabular form using photocopied sheets. Do not neglect to involve pupils in their own assessments of their work and progress. This can be achieved for even the very young by discussion, pupil-review and by inviting comments. Later, children can engage in group discussion offering reasoned arguments about their own and their peers' work. Older pupils should be encouraged to write about what they have done and are quite capable of producing their own 'knowledge/experience webs'. Such pupil self-evaluation should be fixed to the first-hand evidence and kept in each pupil's folio for future reference.

Photography offers a sensible, manageable approach to the recording of practical work. When it is linked to adequate documentary systems and selective procedures for collecting and keeping examples of pupils' work, it can show both the process (through all the stages in production and classroom activities) and the product.

Other ways of record-keeping include the use of annotated 'transfiles' and the use of illustrated pupils' logs. A transfile is a carefully structured collection of annotated first-hand evidence held in a folio which is transferred to the pupil's secondary school – thereby giving a full account of the pupil's practical educational history.

You may also find an annual attainment target matrix which contains reference to ATs and PoS useful for planning and evaluating. On page 29 is a simple matrix that includes the two components and five ATs for design and technology and IT.

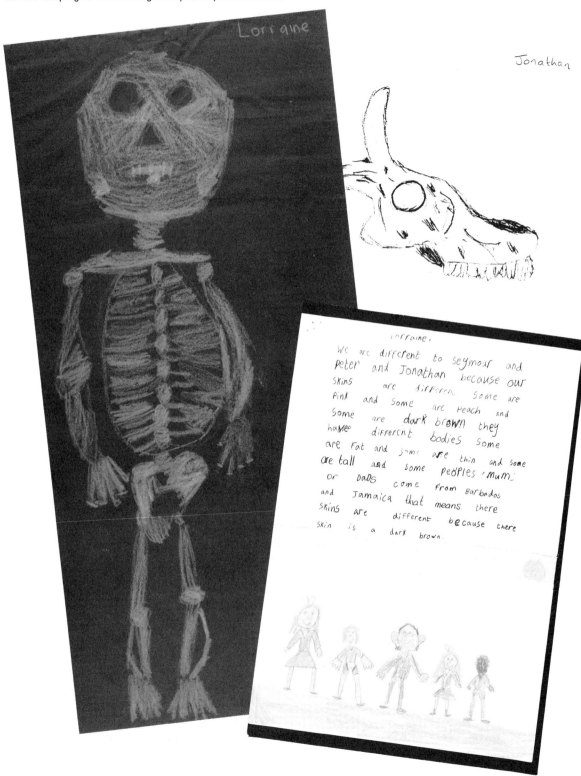

Lorraine

Jonathan

lorraine.

We are different to seymour and peter and Jonathan because our skins are different some are pink and some are peach and some are dark brown they have different bodies some are fat and some are thin and some are tall and some peoples mum or dads come from Barbados and Jamaica that means there skins are different because there skin is a dark brown.

Design and Technology

Teacher's name:_____

Part A	AT1	AT2	AT3	AT4	AT5
Year group					
Levels planned					
Topic titles, dates & durations					

Part B	Contexts	Materials	Concepts	Artefacts/ Systems, etc
Year group				
Levels planned				
Topic titles, dates & durations				

The table on page 29 also shows how you can plan a year's topics. You may wish to modify the matrix to suit yourself. You can now plan to cover the various attainment targets at specific levels. This one form will allow you to record a considerable amount of information. By putting into the relevant boxes the levels which you wish to cover during the various topics, you have, at a glance, a good idea of your year's work for design and technology. As you progress you can tick each box and make appropriate comments as the need arises.

Pupils' record sheets Pupils' record sheets will need to reflect the overall aims of your schemes of work for the year and should be updated every half term. Noteworthy events occur all the time in classrooms; if you use the SoA as the unit for recording (and assessment) you will save time. The documentation suggested below includes elements derived from the programmes of study for key stages 1 and 2:

● Developing and using systems
● Working with materials
● Developing and communicating ideas
● Identifying and satisfying human needs
● IT.

We recommend that you use forms such as that outlined in the next column.

Each pupil's record sheet will need to be cross-referenced to the examples of their first-hand work that is numbered and dated and kept in the transfile or folio. When recording information about SoA and ATs for each pupil it will be necessary to plan your observation of their activities carefully. If pupils are working in groups then use those groups in turn and focus upon those ATs and SoA that you have previously identified for the topic being undertaken. Review sessions with pupils so that they are all involved in a positive way in the recording processes.

Sample Pupil Record for Design and Technology

	level 1	level 2	level 3	level 4	level 5
AT1					
AT2					
AT3					
AT4					
AT5					

has had experience of

understands

assessed as satisfactory using TA

assessed as satisfactory using SAT

Collecting first-hand evidence Remember that first-hand evidence reveals more about the strategies that your pupils have used and about the skills they have employed and developed. It reduces subjectivity, can preserve intermediate stages (thus showing evolution of ideas) and can save (through photographs) otherwise ephemeral kit constructions. This sort of evidence can also preserve large or 'disposable' items, and it reveals much about 'process' as well as the end-product and can involve pupils' assessment in a positive way.

You should therefore certainly collect written and graphic work; if you believe that a piece of work would justify a claim that a particular pupil had satisfied a specific SoA, then the simplest way of recording the fact is to fix to it a dated annotation.

You will need evidence that shows pupils have been able to:

● Generate design specifications and explore ideas
● Identify and clearly state needs

- Make artefacts, systems and environments
- Prepare and work to a plan identifying, managing and using appropriate resources, including knowledge and processes.

Here again you will collect written evidence, plans, designs and finished work.

You will need evidence that shows pupils have been able to develop, communicate and act upon an evaluation of the processes, products and effects of their design and technological activities and of those of others, including those from other times and cultures. You will need written evidence, plans, designs and finished work.

You will also need evidence that shows how pupils have been able to use information technology. As part of first-hand evidence you need to collect three-dimensional work, plans and photographs. Storing three-dimensional work is a problem. Cardboard models can be opened out flat for storage; however, most work will need to be recorded photographically. Photographs need to be taken with care and should be numbered for ease of reference.

It is worth remembering that while it is the quality of the pupil's work and progress that needs to be monitored, the record itself should be of a uniform high quality, otherwise comparisons and judgements will not be soundly based.

Assessment

Why do we assess?

Formal requirements for assessment have developed from the very natural desires of parents, pupils and teachers to know how well pupils are progressing. Assessment also has a formative role in feeding-back information to teachers about the best ways to go about improving their teaching strategies.

The general purposes behind assessment are said to be to raise standards and improve performance in scientific and technological areas. The Education Reform Act requires that at the end or near the end of each key stage it is necessary to:

> *"Ascertain what pupils have achieved in relation to the attainment targets for that stage."*
> Technology in the National Curriculum (DES, HMSO. 1990)

The emphasis for assessment is on achievement. When assessments are made at key stage 1 you will not be required to include examinations and tests however you should ensure that you make proper provision for SATs through your continuous programme of teacher assessment.

Avoid the trap of thinking of design and technology as simply craft design and technology (CDT) with the addition of home economics and information technology capability. Do not dwell on past vocational strategies of previous generations but look forward to the skills and processes that are beyond the craft skills of working wood, metal and fabric.

Teacher assessment (TA)

It is certain that the role of continuous teacher assessment (TA) is vital in providing information for future stages of individual pupils' development. The importance of TA will grow as it is increasingly seen as a reliable and manageable approach to assessment. The statements of attainment can be seen as adding clarity for teachers undertaking their assessment of pupils' achievements:

> *" Children should know when, and what they have achieved."*
> ibid.

The SEAC pack includes useful information and a number of helpful examples. We recommend that your work as assessor be set within a whole school policy on assessment. The development of such a policy should be part of a continuous process of review and development of school and individual teachers' educational capability.

If planning and assessment are approached positively you will be able to:

- Make an appropriate teaching plan
- Identify what is noteworthy
- Identify what pupils should do next.

We should be probing the quality and the development of pupils' thinking through the interaction between the hand and mind and we should scrutinise examples of pupils' work for evidence that helps us to assess both the process and product. This evidence is naturally in the form of designs, sketches, plans, notes and models that represent the pupils' attempts to engage their creative speculations with the material world.

You will also be able to:

- Help improve your own teaching skills
- Monitor the progress of your pupils
- Produce reports for various audiences, including parents.

You need not abandon your own teaching style (under the weight of extra burdens and a perceived easier option of an assessment-led curriculum).

Managing assessment

There are two main elements to consider:

- What to assess
- How to assess practical activities.

Design and technology is a new curriculum area and as such it will provoke discussion amongst your colleagues. These should lead

to the designation of a design and technology co-ordinator. Such a co-ordinator will be responsible for the day-to-day implementation of technology policy, including:

- Co-ordination
- Resources
- Staff development and support
- Review
- External liaison.

Planning for assessment

The design and technology co-ordinator will need to work closely with other members of staff on planning, and in particular with the school co-ordinator for assessment. This should include the development of short, medium and long-term planning and the writing of an overall assessment policy document which includes particular reference to design and technology.

Planning for assessment ought to include strategies to:

- Provide colleagues with information
- Ensure consistency of approach throughout the school
- Provide regular opportunities for evaluation and action
- Develop moderation
- Write an assessment policy document.

Establishing good practice

The first thing to be said about establishing good practice is that there is plenty of evidence that an abundance of teachers in primary schools are well qualified to link the requirements of the National Curriculum with their own well-developed preferred approaches. In fact, primary teachers are in many cases already expert assessors.

Our experience has been that design and technology activities are often best organised with groups of pupils working on aspects of a cross-curricular topic and differentiated by activity, materials or tools and equipment. The obvious practical benefits of this approach are spelled out in the chapter on organisation and management (Chapter 3). For assessment it will allow you to follow a normal approach to classroom management while concentrating on the achievements of a selected group of pupils for specific SoA in a variety of curricular areas.

What and how to assess

The assessment of achievement in design and technology will include product and process. The attainment targets describe 'process' skills while the programmes of study include particular aspects of knowledge which may or may not be tested in the formal assessments (SATs). While it is clear that the individual statements of attainment will be the main element for assessment, you know that in a busy primary classroom, children are simultaneously achieving a large number of attainment targets – and that trying to monitor all of this is impossible and unnecessary. As many of the attainment targets in design and technology (and English and mathematics) result in 'products', assessment of these can take place after they are completed. However, it is essential that these products should be sampled on a regular and consistent basis and assessed every half term.

Products The changes in the kinds of activities that are involved in design and technology over old CDT extend the kinds of products that need to be assessed. Evidence of all attainment targets will be gathered, including artefacts, systems, and environments.

These will be supported by evidence of written plans/evaluations, sketches, plans and models, and will be made with a variety of materials.

Processes The range of processes to be assessed will include:

- Investigating
- Devising
- Gathering information
- Selecting
- Exploring
- Imagining
- Generating ideas
- Using information
- Identifying needs and opportunities
- Organising
- Explaining
- Sharing/cooperating
- Recording
- Predicting
- Reflecting and refining
- Analysing patterns (IT)
- Designing
- Making.

How to assess

Ensure that you do not follow practices that might tend to label children as failures. We all know that children develop at different rates, and have different strengths and weaknesses at different ages. Assessment, if used appropriately, can help them to become aware of their individual strengths and can motivate them towards improvement in achievement.

Reflect upon your skills that might aid assessment. Do you question in an open or closed way? Asking children questions will help you to assess what they know and their stages in conceptual development. However you will need to ask all your children, otherwise this may prove to be a biased and unreliable method of assessment.

Do you keep a regularly updated log or diary for recording what is noteworthy?

Using a diary on a regular basis will allow you to note the growth points in pupils' knowledge, understanding and skill that have been described in statements of attainment. In such a diary you should note:

- What you have observed
- What you have heard
- When any noteworthy events occurred.

Assessing products   The assessment of two- and three-dimensional products from design and technology activities needs careful planning. As with all subjects, it is not the intention that teachers should assess every statement of attainment by testing pupils. You will need to sample. For your sampling you need to follow a systematic approach that will form part of sampling activities for core and foundation subjects.

How to scrutinise and judge pupils' practical work   It is very important to try to differentiate elements of the work that you are judging. You may find that by producing a simple assessment form you always have a checklist of such elements with which to work. See page 35 for a suggested layout.

The items that are kept as evidence should be numbered, (use a child's initials to prefix a running number), dated and the level and relevant ATs noted. You may wish to mark work; we would suggest that if you do so, you relate marks to the ATs. Make sure that the marks you make mean the same to your pupils as they do to you. It is also important that work is reviewed with the individual pupils and marked together, if possible. This will help assessment to be formative and will help inform pupils about your expectations.

You will be able to timetable review sessions more easily if your pupils are also involved in the 'sifting' processes of products, so that you keep only those items that are useful for the education of your pupils.

Assessing processes   Some of the processes listed above, particularly those that relate to designing and making, can be assessed from the evidence collected in the form of products. You may also find some evidence of generating ideas, identifying needs and opportunities in the sample of products that you have sifted and collected.

Others, however, will have to be assessed 'in action'. You will need to observe and assess other processes as they happen in class. The processes that need to be assessed in this way are:

- Gathering information
- Selecting
- Exploring
- Imagining
- Using information
- Organising
- Explaining
- Sharing
- Co-operating.

Other processes can be assessed from the self-evaluation that your pupils should undertake. Such self-evaluation should be the concluding phase of each design process cycle and would often be a written, brief account of what your pupils have done. The processes that will often be covered in such accounts can include:

- Investigating
- Devising
- Gathering information
- Selecting
- Imagining
- Generating ideas
- Using information
- Identifying needs
- Identifying opportunities
- Organising
- Explaining
- Recording
- Reflecting and refining.

Being fair Within your school policy on assessment you need to address the problems of objective assessment. Strictly speaking there is nothing truly 'objective' – we can only hope to approach objectivity. We do so by having our own personal views validated in a wider public. Here is the clue to ensuring greater fairness in your assessments. It may be worth integrating some or all of the following points within your own school policy:

- Regularly have your assessments and marks validated by your colleagues in 'blind tests'
- Use standard approaches and checklists
- Design and use stationery for your internal teacher assessment
- Involve pupils in assessment processes.

Sample Annual Practical Activities Record Form – two- and three- dimensional (including written)

Name:_____   Class:_____

Two-dimensional work				
Date & item number	Type of product	Accuracy/ Appropriateness	Detail/ Finish	Aesthetic/ Creative
date: number: AT & level:				
date: number: AT & level:				
date: number: AT & level:				
date: number: AT & level:				

Three-dimensional work				
Date & item number	Type of product	Accuracy/ Appropriateness	Detail/ Finish	Aesthetic/ Creative
date: number: AT & level:				
date: number: AT & level:				
date: number: AT & level:				
date: number: AT & level:				

3

ORGANISING AND MANAGING DESIGN AND TECHNOLOGY

This chapter provides ideas about how to organise and manage practical activities and resources in your school and classroom. We offer advice on the range of school resources that will be needed within any medium-size primary school.

You will need to organise the classroom, your resources and your pupils, to allow for:

- A variety of ways of working with your pupils
- A number of different activities
- Individual, group and class work.

You will have to organise and manage your pupils and classroom, materials and equipment, time, and, quite possibly, your own professional practice within a whole-school approach. In the practical consideration of these you will, of course, have to take account of the need for structured progression of educational opportunities and the requirements of the National Curriculum.

Organising staff

Design and technology is a relatively new curriculum area and many staff will therefore be in need of the help and support of a co-ordinator. The coordinator will have the responsibility for the day-to-day implementation of the school policy for design and technology. In particular the elements of managing design and technology listed below will fall to the coordinator.

The role of the coordinator

- *Reviewing present practice*
  - *reviewing technology provision in the school*
  - *involving all the staff in review*
- *Staff development and support*
  - *assisting in the development of schemes of work for different year groups*
  - *arranging in-service support*
  - *providing advice*
  - *working with staff to improve practice*
- *Resources*
  - *advising on resources*
  - *advising on health and safety*
- *Coordination*
  - *ensuring consistent approaches across the school*
  - *establishing continuity between year groups*
  - *working with others, advising on assessing and recording*
- *External liaison*
  - *keeping up-to-date*
  - *liaising with LEA and other advisory services.*

Organising your classroom

Classroom requirements

Design and technology requires a mixed teaching style and this in turn will affect the way that you organise your classroom. There will be much emphasis on investigative work in which children are effectively in charge of their own learning. Your role in the classroom will constantly change in response to this and there will need to be frequent opportunities for group work.

As you introduce design and technology activities into your schemes of work, one of the first considerations will be to define the kinds of activities that are likely to be involved and how you will organise your pupils, from reception classes through to top juniors. What are the implications for the layout of your classroom? The kinds of contact that teachers need to have with their children include guiding, demonstrating, questioning, informing and working alongside. These types of contact will help your pupils to work co-operatively and independently. Such varied contact will require you to make provision in your classroom for individual, pair, group and whole class work.

You will also need to cater for different activities such as quiet study, discussion, planning and review, practical work and drama. The physical organisation of your classroom needs careful consideration; areas need to be clearly defined so that your children know how to work in each section, and how to care for and tidy each area. Obviously your classroom has its own limitations of shape, size, light and design. Nevertheless it may be a good idea for you to reassess the situation with the aim of using what you have to the best advantage. Make a plan (or, if you have the time and inclination, a scale model) of your classroom, furniture and equipment. This will be a great help when re-planning your layout.

A rich and stimulating environment is essential

37

Do not overlook the need to make your classroom and school a rich and stimulating environment. It is very important to make displays that include stimulating resources and carefully-mounted children's work. Using artefacts, models and museum specimens linked carefully with appropriate books, prints and posters will give an exciting atmosphere as a background to, and source for, high quality educational experiences. Such displays will enhance and support your pupils' understanding that there are no rigid boundaries between areas of knowledge, and will help encourage understanding of concepts of pattern, texture, shape, form and structure that are common to design and technology, science, mathematics and art.

Besides developing and using your own school resource centre do not forget to use the services from central museums and libraries. Children should also be encouraged to bring things in from home so that they can take an active role in the design of displays and resourcing of their classroom. Because of the length of time it takes to complete models and other products of practical activities it will be very useful to create a space where partly complete models can be placed either for storage or as a working display.

Furniture Each school building is different, with its own strong points and limitations. Even taking account of the differences it is true that often there is too much furniture in classrooms and this makes it difficult to demarcate various working areas. Like any other activity, planning your classroom will need to be based upon a good understanding of your resources and needs. Besides areas for discussion and review you will have two main requirements. These are for a practical area and a study/reading area.

An area for practical activities You will understand the need for a specific well-defined and equipped area for practical activities. This area will be somewhere children can work with materials that may be messy, away from their other work and with a feeling of confidence and security.

It is essential that you arrange for resources to be well labelled and that each has its own storage location. Your children should maintain the area and this will help them develop a sense of responsibility and pride. Resources and tools that are available should be relevant to the age-range and the children's skill and ability to use them properly and safely. Floor and work surfaces should be suitable for the types of activities involved.

The following kinds of work require some special provisions.

Clay work

This is best done on absorbent surfaces. If a polythene or vinyl table is used more mess will be made when the clay dries and flakes off. Card, wooden or hardboard are best.

Art, design and textile work

Painting should be done on an easily wipeable surface, or on an absorbent surface such as newspaper. Easels are not really appropriate as young children find it awkward to paint at arm's length. Also, thin paint will tend to run and frustrate children's efforts. Charcoal, pastels, felt-tip pen and pencil drawings can all be made on a flat dry surface. Working with textiles will usually require a clean flat surface.

Construction

Work using wood, card, metal, plastic, glues and pins or nails will require the use of a strong bench or workstation preferably fitted with a vice for holding the material safely for cutting, shaping, drilling and finishing. If you have not got a bench, then an old and substantial wooden table will suffice as long as it is sturdy enough to allow hammering and sawing in safety.

Food

It is most desirable for schools to provide a central site specifically for activities with food. Food surfaces must be kept clean, hygienic and away from other materials. Thorough preparation of work surfaces and implements must take place before working with foodstuffs.

Study/quiet area If you have made a plan of your classroom (and corridors) you may be able to identify an area that could be designated as a book corner. This will provide an area where children can retreat if they want to read either for recreation or research. A reading corner needs to be attractive, inviting, stimulating and conducive to relaxed reading. You may find that your local library service will be able to help organise exchanges of books so that your own collection can be supplemented and enriched on a regular basis.

Reading areas can be made inviting and attractive with cushions and toys. You can match the progress of topics by arranging weekly displays of books and artefacts. Don't miss the opportunity to include questions in your displays.

Displays should also include books that have been made by your children: their own dictionaries, story books, logs and invention books.

Include questions in your displays

The organisation, storage and maintenance of materials, kits, tools and equipment is vital. It is through their use and understanding that the important skills and concepts of design and technology are developed. A wide variety of resources is essential for providing quality learning experiences. Materials, tools and equipment should be readily available for construction, textile work, art and design and food studies to support pupils' progressional needs. You will find detailed advice on materials, tools and components in Chapter 5.

Some resources will need to be held centrally in your school and some in your own classroom. The way you plan the availability and accessibility of these resources is a matter that needs the consideration of a whole school plan. Strategies need to be discussed by the whole staff so that a coherent policy for resourcing can be established.

The school's resources should be arranged in terms of:

- Pupils' age-range
- Pupils' ability, skills and knowledge
- Health and safety
- Hygiene.

Also you need to decide which 'precious or dangerous' resources such as cameras, cutting tools and valuable materials should be held centrally. It is a good idea to hold tools together not in a central cupboard but in a mobile work station and tool store. If you wish to house your tools in a mobile unit such as the 'Techcart', decide whether or not you simply want a small mobile tool box or a full size work station with variable height; then compare prices, taking into account the facilities offered and your needs.

Each classroom will need its own allocation of basic materials such as wood, clay, card, fabrics, graphic materials and paint. Consideration must be given to how materials are kept in the classroom, where they are stored, their availability and labelling.

Below we offer a breakdown of the resources that will need to be held centrally and those which will be needed by each class. Obviously this is only an indication of the kind of provision you may need to make, and can be supplemented by many other items that can be found in Chapter 5.

An investigative approach to learning will succeed only if it is supported by the necessary learning resources. These need to be an integrated range of books, audio-visual materials, authentic artefacts (from museum services) carefully chosen to be appropriate for your pupils.

Books

Books should stimulate different reading skills: reading for pleasure and research, for information and reference. They should be suitable for the age-range, ability and interests of the children.

First hand resources

There are artefacts and objects which generate first hand experiences of many concepts. You may be able to provide your own collection of interesting objects. Alternatively, you may have a good museum service that will be pleased to help you. Try to ensure that you do not rely only on natural history type specimens. It is essential that you make your displays with a range of artefacts from the man-made world as well. They will stimulate an exciting environment in your classroom. With original materials available you will find that the use of books will be transformed and will encourage children to answer questions about the artefacts.

Team/class resources

work station and tool kits
construction kits
2 vices
G-clamp
set square
hand drill and bits
wooden mallet
hammer
hole punch/drill
surform file and blades
small pliers
2 bench hooks
8 pulleys
2 spring balances
tongs
indoor and outdoor thermometers
pond dippers
various capacity/volume containers
compass
boxes of construction straws
construction kits
balsa wood
cork, wooden and plastic wheels
cotton reels
ping-pong balls
rubber bands
set of small screwdrivers
assorted rubber and plastic tubing
plastic bags
glue gun
sets of magnets (including bar magnets)
hand lenses
batteries
bulbs
bulb holders
switches and bell wire
candles
suckers and springs
metal safety rulers
craft knives
scissors

School resources

sets of metal masses
pulleys
spring balances
micrometer
large pulley
large compass
spirit level
G-clamp
set square
hand drill plus twist bits
hammer
wooden mallet
surform file and blades
hacksaws and spare blades
small and large pliers
pair of tongs
microscope
insect retrievers
transformers
light box
flexi-mirrors
aquaria tanks
glue guns and sticks
stopclocks
Check card
work cards
coloured acetate sheets

When you plan your scheme of work you can make sure that there is a balance of 'man-made' and 'natural' starting points and that your displays match these differences. One week, for example, there could be a display of shells for close observation drawings. This could bring out an understanding of natural structures. The following week could be balanced by a display of machine parts that link with the structural aspects of the shells. Again you have opportunities to include questions as part of the display.

Kits

Educational kits play an important role in children's conceptual and learning-skill development. Ideas can be tried out without the added problems of applying difficult 'making skills'.

It is quite common practice for nursery and infant children to change the identity of their model a number of times in a very short period of time. Even older, more experienced children will frequently change the shape, size and function of a model before arriving at a satisfactory solution. It can be incorrectly assumed that because young children quickly assemble kits into models that move or are articulated, they have formed a firm understanding of these functions. This is a dangerous misconception.

Kit modelling is used best when it is an activity that is carefully balanced with the necessary experiences gained by using a variety of other materials. Kits provide opportunities for children to understand and come to terms with the form and nature of things through play. Ideally, a range of kits should be made available to children. Jumbo kits are particularly valuable for very young children as they can be used to help create imaginative play environments to develop an understanding of spatial relationships, size and shape. They also encourage co-operative play and stimulate interactive skills.

Construction kits, therefore, can play an important part in a child's conceptual and manual development. There is considerable choice for the infant years, where it is possible to select different kits to provide progression. With older children the choice is more limited, but progression may still be achieved through the addition of components which offer greater challenges. The list opposite is arranged to help you to plan progression. At the very earliest years we have found that Bauspiel/Bauplay is particularly good as it comprises large colourful well-manufactured components that can be used in a variety of ways. Fischertechnik is excellent and is available in special large quantities for class use. Other kits that can be recommended are also included in the table.

To give you some idea of relative costs, we have included numbers on a scale of 1–14 that relate to the approximate cost of basic quantities of the components: 14 is the most expensive. Kits (apart from Fischertechnik) are stocked by numerous suppliers whose prices can be strikingly different; it is wise to check prices before placing orders. The list includes a basic description for kits where we felt this to be appropriate; the majority are plastic with various methods of fixing.

Some kits offer accessories as extras to enhance imaginative opportunities for pupils. Some suppliers and manufacturers offer a spares service to replace lost items or increase the number of a particular component to cover against loss of these items.

In Chapter 5 an outline of the resources you will need is provided in a comprehensive account of components, materials and tools.

A comparative chart of construction kits

Kit	Range	Price guide *	Description/uses/drawbacks
Wooden	KS1 – KS2	3/4	Traditional, easy to use versatile blocks
Bauplay	KS1 – KS2	10	Large colourful components, ideal for the earliest years
Basic Builder	KS1 – KS2	1	Inexpensive, rather limited
TacTic	KS1 – KS2	5	Large scale components that lock together, strong enough to sit on
Mobilo	KS1 – KS2	3	Very good plastic – suitable for pre-school
Playmobile	KS1 – KS2	3	Excellent for pre-school and later
Duplo	KS1 – KS2	3	Wide age-range – from 18 months to 10 or 11 years. Useful additional features including zoos and houses. Quite small, so supervision of young children is necessary
Lasy	KS1 – KS2	3	Plastic, durable, good for imaginative work
Mini Quadro	KS1 – KS2	8	Basic, a little stiff for younger fingers
Quadro	KS1 – KS3	14	Challenging, large construction kits that can be made up into climbing frames, etc
Construx	KS1 – KS2	3	OK for top infants; not a first choice
Meccano	KS1 – KS3	3	Well-known pioneer in construction kits
Lego	KS1 – KS3	4	Favourite with plenty of additional features
Lego Technic	KS2 – KS3	8	Includes computer control systems
Lego Dacta	KS2 – KS3	8	Computer packages for Lego Technic kits
Fischertechnik	KS2 – KS4	4	Available now for top infants and up through the levels to key stage 4
Polydron	KS1 – KS2	6	Exceptional construction kits: the flexible net systems that can be rolled up into solids are particularly good for relating 2D and 3D space

On a scale 1–14, where 14 is most expensive

4

A TOPIC BANK FOR DESIGN AND TECHNOLOGY

The aim of this chapter is to provide you with a useable ideas bank of topic-based activities for design and technology at both key stages, which can either be used 'off the peg' or adapted to meet your own needs. It may also be used as a model for different types of topic planning and applied to your own, different topics.

Why work from topics?

You will find it valuable to consider a topic-based approach to technology for two principle reasons:

- The practical problem of fitting in all of the new National Curriculum requirements make a cross-curricular approach extremely time-effective
- Design and technology, unlike other more content-based subjects, is very suitable for a cross-curricular topic approach.

The very nature of design and technology is cross-curricular. Technology is very strongly linked to science and mathematics and has so many processes in common with English, geography and history that it can be rightly seen as a hub to a wheel of educational activities. A cross-curricular topic approach is valuable because of the power of design and technology as the practical 'yeast' for many subjects. Through a practical approach, science and technology become much easier

to understand. This crucial role of design and technology is stated:

> " *Pupils should draw on their knowledge and skills in other subjects, particularly the foundation subjects of science, mathematics and art, to support their designing and making activities.* "
>
> *Technology in the National Curriculum* (DES, HMSO. 1990)

We believe that, in practice, it will not normally be necessary to think up new topics for design and technology. However it is necessary to ensure balance between 'natural and man-made' starting points in your cross-curricular planning.

Links with other subjects

Science Technology uses the methodology of science and relies to a large extent for its development on scientific knowledge; in turn it has equipped and fostered the development of science. The National Curriculum Science Working Group pointed to the long-established links between technology and science.

> " *During its history, science has drawn on technology in developing its instrumentation and techniques of enquiry. Significant discoveries have depended on the development of particular tools, materials and techniques. Conversely, in attempting to solve a problem to meet a need, whether it is designing a bridge*

for a particular site or finding ways of providing human communities with clean drinking water, technologists may draw on and use scientific knowledge."

Science for Ages 5-16 (HMSO. 1988)

Just as in the wider world, scientific and technological activities are mutually supportive in the classroom. When engaged in design and technological activities, pupils will draw upon appropriate scientific skills and knowledge to help solve their problems and produce solutions.

Mathematics The links with mathematics are clear. The Cockcroft report (1982) stated:

"*Most children learn mathematics most effectively when they learn it through practical activities.*"

Activities such as measuring, estimating and calculating are central to design and technology. Concepts such as symmetry, pattern and shape find their practical expression through design and technology.

History and geography History and geography will provide many opportunities for design and technology. Comparing basic human needs and solutions with the same needs in other times and cultures will give children opportunities to engage in wide-ranging technological activities. The topics in the topic bank on Wheels at key stage 2 and Structures at key stage 1 are good examples of how you can link history with technology.

Art and design In the early years of schooling, art and design play an essential part in

Children can help structure your topic through discussion

the development of children's language and making skills. Through drawing and painting, children are able to name and describe their experience of the world and thus to strengthen their use of language. Through working with a variety of materials children are able to refine and extend their designing and making skills and to lay the foundation for technical accomplishment.

The development of drawing skills provides children with an essential means of observing, recording and analysing the appearance and structure of the real world. Such skills are valuable in their own right and also contribute significantly to other curricular areas where the ability to investigate and respond to evidence through drawing is essential.

Common processes

You will know from your own personal knowledge that there are many processes that are shared by design and technology, information technology, science, maths, English and other subject areas. These activities represent some of the range:

- Co-operating/collaborating
- Taking responsibility
- Exploring
- Asking questions
- Investigating
- Reflecting
- Choosing and decision making
- Imagining
- Organising
- Monitoring
- Explaining
- Recording
- Communicating/talking
- Interpreting
- Sharing
- Predicting
- Observing
- Recalling.

What kind of topics?

You will need to provide topics of different types and durations, along the lines of the following:

Mini-topics Commonly these are problem-solving activities that last for short periods of time – sometimes measured in hours rather than days. Time and resources may be specified as part of the 'brief'.

Short term Some topics or projects are concentrated short-term activities, (up to a week) that emphasise one area of the curriculum. Other short topics may involve more curricular areas. Some of the examples in the topic bank, such as the Problem-solving topics, and Celebrations at KS2, are of this type.

Longer topics Other topics have extended time-scales and commonly last for half or a full term. The majority of the topics in the topic bank are of this type. These extended projects often develop in a somewhat organic way and almost certainly will include mini-topics as part of their development. These will arise naturally as part of an investigative approach to learning.

Starting points for topics Each teacher titles her topics or themes in a descriptive way so that a central core forms a hub from which related ideas radiate. We know that some teachers have tended to use 'brainstorming' exercises to generate breathtaking extensions of central ideas. Uncontrolled brainstorming can result in a lack of structure and thorough planning. Often topic plans from such approaches contain unrelated and ill-considered elements. You will find that the topics in the next section are all structured to provide coverage of clearly-identified elements of the National Curriculum attainment targets and programmes of study.

A topic bank for primary schools

This section of the book provides ten double topics. Each topic contains ideas and activities at key stage 1 and key stage 2 and provides a progression of concepts, activities and materials. The topics are:

Pirates and treasure islands
Problem solving
Celebrations
Transport
Conservation
Wheels
Structures
Food
The post
Clothes.

Each topic starts from the design cycle and attainment targets as outlined on page 3, and identifies clearly the National Curriculum coverage of the topics and the links within the wider curriculum. You will find that not all the topics start from *Identify needs and opportunities*. In line with the intentions of National Curriculum, they start at different points within the whole cycle; these starting points are indicated with a framed box.

Most of the topics provide up to half a term's activity. Others, such as Problem solving, are intended to provide short-term 'mini-topics'. Some are smaller parts of larger topics, others are all-embracing. You will find too that different key stages will sometimes approach a topic in completely different ways and provide examples of progression in action as outlined in Chapter 2.

The aim of this diversity is to provide you with a bank of materials that introduce you to all the different ways of developing wide-ranging technology through topic work. You can use the topics as 'off the peg' resources for the key stage you teach, adapt them to the needs of your own particular situation or use them as models for developing your own schemes of work with a different set of topics.

Used in their own right, these topics can provide a complex scheme of work at each key stage. Together the topics provide a resource that covers all parts of the attainment targets and programmes of study for the design and technology profile component, as well as a wide range of contexts and a mixture of outcomes (artefacts, systems and environments).

Design and Technology Web – Pirates and treasure islands KS 1

Identify needs and opportunities

- This will consist mainly in linking appropriate solutions to the perceived needs and opportunities that are contained in the set tasks

Generate designs

- For structures to live in
- For a wall frieze
- For a treasure chest
- For a vehicle to travel across various surfaces
- For a device to collect coconuts

Design and Technology Cycle

Evaluate

- All items under generating designs and planning and making

Plan and make

- Pirate boats and ships
- A model of the island
- Clay figureheads
- A treasure chest
- A device to collect coconuts

National Curriculum coverage in design and technology

Design cycle phases

- **Identifying needs and opportunities** Limited scope

- **Generating designs** Considerable scope for two-dimensional and three-dimensional design stages

- **Planning and making** Structures to live in on the island, a treasure chest, a vehicle which can travel across sand, marsh and woods. Treasure maps and treasure trails. A device to get a coconut down from a tree. A model of the island and clay figureheads for the ship. The pirate ship and boats

- **Evaluating** Continual process for all products

The programme of study

- **Developing and using artefacts, systems and environments** In addition to those listed under *Planning and making* it is possible to consider the problems of desert island environments and designing ways of solving the agricultural difficulties. Making a chest from an old shoe box can involve making mechanisms for opening, closing and locking

- **Working with materials** Clay, plastic bottles, plasticine kits, balsa wood, card, paper, graphic materials, fabrics

- **Developing and communicating ideas**

- **Satisfying needs and addressing opportunities**

Cross-curricular coverage

- **English** Writing stories

- **Music** Pirate songs

- **Information technology** Using programmes such as *Fairy Tales* to make up stories

- **Mathematics** Measuring, estimating

- **Science** Floating and sinking, recognising important similarities and differences such as hardness, flexibility and transparency in the characteristics of materials

- **Art** Painting and decorating a variety of models and objects. Designing and making a wall frieze

Introduction

This is a topic that offers a tremendous range of design and technology activities. Young children are fascinated by stories of rough old seadogs, gold, silver and chests of jewels. They love playing games and acting out self-invented stories based on books and cartoons such as the *Bobobobs*.

Getting started

Following storytelling sessions and group discussions the activities listed form the

framework for a topic planned to run for six weeks.

Resources and classroom organisation

Having identified a good spread of activities children can be divided into groups to undertake the tasks at different times. Computers and software such as *Fairy Tales* will be needed; if you do not have ready access to these, contact your specialist computer or primary adviser for help before starting the topic. Over the six weeks a full range of art, design and craft materials and tools will be used, including clay, plasticine, paper, card (Checkcard will be very useful), junk materials (tubes, shoe boxes and cardboard boxes), plastic bottles (for ships) and other junk plastics, and kits such as Lego, Bauplay and Fischertechnik. Felt-tip pens, paint, pencils, scissors and safety snips, fabric scraps, threads, beads and sequins (for collage work) will also be necessary.

Activities

All of the activities to some extent involve designing and making.

The first activity, writing a story and storing it by using a computer programme, will help children link the use of computers and the more practical aspects of solving the problems of pirates and treasure-hunters.

Map reading will be a necessary activity to arrive at the treasure island and then to secure the buried treasure. However, before looking for the hiding place the primary objective will be to build a secure place to live. During this activity it will be appropriate to ask questions:

● Where should you build your shelter?
● Does it need to be fortified?
● What will it be made from?
● What happens if it rains: will you and your stores be dry?
● Where will you store your treasure?

Designing and making a treasure chest can combine technological skills and mechanisms with aesthetic considerations.

Children can be faced with the problem of travelling around the island, with its variety of terrains. The first task is that of imagining the kinds of difficulties that are likely to be faced. Children's imaginations are fired by authentic and second-hand experiences.

Books that deal with different environments, visits to geological sites and examinations of soils, sands and peat will all be useful. Designing a vehicle to cope with different surfaces on the island after such preparation will be a greatly enhanced activity.

Securing adequate fresh food supplies will be very important. Here the problems of scurvy and health for early seafarers can form the centre of a mini-topic with a number of possible design and technology activities, for example a device to collect coconuts.

Planning and making pirate boats and ships will involve concepts such as floating, sinking, stability, balance, volume, area, size and capacity. Using squared paper and Checkcard will enable children to work easily from small to big and from two to three dimensions.

Making a model of the island can involve building up layers of clay to make a contoured model that can, when dry, be painted. The models will be useful when designing vehicles to cross the island and for planning treasure trails and safe harbours and sites for shelters. Figureheads can be carved from balsa wood or modelled from plasticine or clay and fixed to the pirate ships prior to decoration. Here is an opportunity of ensuring that the scale of the pirate's ship matches that of the figurehead.

Recording

Photography will be important to record the stages in designing and making activities. Plans on paper and card can be annotated and filed away for future reference. Likewise written stories, poems and songs can be annotated and filed in the children's individual folios. As in all recording activities you will need to work with the children to be selective so that you do not end up with a huge pile of disorganised information.

Pirates and treasure islands key stage 2

Design and Technology Web – Pirates and treasure Islands KS 2

Identify needs and opportunities

Problem-solving activities based upon computer program
- To find route to island
- To find and recover treasure
- Map making and interpretation
- Make a game based on pirates

Design and Technology Cycle

Evaluate
- Success of routes
- Success of keys/maps
- The games

Generate designs
- Using grid patterns
- Using maps and keys
- Using a game on pirates
- Modify computer programs

Plan and make
- Routes to the island and treasure
- Maps and keys to the maps
- A game based on stories about pirates

National Curriculum coverage in design and technology

Design cycle phases

- **Identifying needs and opportunities** The 'set-problem' nature of the topic defines needs and opportunities

- **Designing** Excellent wide ranging design activities utilising manual and computer skills. Taking original programs – changing them, designing game boards, graphics, maps, symbols

- **Making** Mock-ups and final games, maps and modified computer programs

- **Evaluating** Children are able to evaluate their success in finding routes and can test their ideas for symbols on their friends. When they design games there are many opportunities to see how good they are

The programme of study

- **Developing and using artefacts, systems and environments** Artefacts and systems are covered: 1) maps, 2) computer programs and games

- **Working with materials** Graphic materials, paper, card, plastics

- **Developing and communicating ideas** Great scope including creative writing, giving instructions, producing viable symbols and graphic imagery, mapping skills

- **Satisfying needs and addressing opportunities** A specific requirement is that pupils solve problems

Cross-curricular coverage

- **English** Creative writing opportunities, e.g. 'How I got shipwrecked', 'Alone on the island', 'Finding the treasure'. Oral work, e.g. giving instructions to complete computer program, discussion over designs for games and writing instructions for the games

- **Information technology** Using and modifying programs

- **Mathematics** Measuring, gridwork, symmetry

- **Geography** Mapwork, orientation

- **Science** Weather and the use of stars for navigation

Introduction

This topic is designed to last approximately six weeks and focusses on the use of computers. It is most appropriate at the top of key stage 2.

Getting started

It would be particularly suitable to introduce the topic by reading from *Treasure Island* or other pirate stories. After this we recommend that your point of departure should be the use of a computer program on treasure islands. Such programs involve finding an island and subsequently the treasure. Children can deal with choices, making deci-

sions and modifying plans and directions and logical approaches to complex problems. This well-structured introduction to the topic can then be linked with imaginative activities that could include drama events based on stories involving pirates and the other activities listed below. It is recommended that prior to undertaking this topic some time is devoted to developing the children's skills in writing simple programs.

Resources and classroom organisation

You will need computers, printers and appropriate software (if you do not have suitable programs it should be possible to find someone willing to write one or two for you). A supply of Checkpaper, card, paints, felt-tip pens and drawing equipment, maps, model pirate boats, costumes, cutlasses and books will be useful.

Activities

The activities will be:

- Using and modifying computer programs
- Writing stories/plays and acting out dramatic events
- Designing and making games on the theme of pirates. Writing the rules for the games
- Designing and making maps with keys and instructions to enable the treasure to be found.

In the first activity children can use and develop their computer logic skills in seeking the location of treasure. Do not miss opportunities for asking questions about why children follow particular paths. Children will be involved in selecting, deciding, reviewing and eventually modifying programs. Such modifications may be simply the relocation of the position of treasure or a wholesale redesigning of the program. Such redesigned programs can then be used by other children to test their deductive skills.

When children come to write stories and plays they will use their experience of the program. They may produce more complex stories than previously. They may map out the structure of stories before writing them.

If you add an additional requirement that needs to be satisfied when designs for the games are produced, such as 'all games must be useful in teaching adding and subtraction', then this activity will have more meaning. Such a requirement will also make games easier to evaluate. We suggest that

you ask your pupils to consider the following points:

- What is the object of the game?
- How many players can play the game at the same time?
- Will it be a card game or board game (or combination of the two)?
- What graphic images might need to be repeated (such as a pirate's head or Jolly Roger sign)?
- How to produce the game, whether it needs to be protected by laminating, for example
- How to write clear simple instructions.

The final activity of designing and making a pirate treasure map will have been set up by the previous activities. Questions to raise might include:

- How old is the map supposed to be?
- How can it made to look old?
- How will you know which way to go?
- How will you know how far to go?
- How will you recognise features such as trees, cliffs and so on?
- How much food might be needed to go so far?

By displaying different examples of maps from those of Ptolemy, Copernicus, Speed, underground maps and even plans of printed circuits you will greatly widen the experiences of your pupils.

Recording

If children make changes to computer programs, try to 'screen-dump' to produce a print. This can then be marked up and saved in folios with their other work. Involve the children in selecting work to be annotated, dated and stored for future reference. If games are three-dimensional it may be worth taking photographs or otherwise saving the two-dimensional plans and sketches.

Problem solving key stage 1

Design and Technology Web – Problem solving KS 1

Identify needs and opportunities
- Set tasks

Evaluate
- A moving teddy
- A see-saw
- A junk robot with working lights

Design and Technology Cycle

Generate designs
- For a moving teddy
- For a see-saw
- For a junk robot with working lights

Plan and make
- A moving teddy
- A see-saw
- A junk robot with working lights

National Curriculum coverage in design and technology

Design cycle phases

- **Identifying needs and opportunities** Limited coverage

- **Generating designs** Express ideas, use talk, pictures, drawing, models to develop designs

- **Planning and making** Use a variety of materials to make simple things, describe what they are doing, improvise

- **Evaluating** Through discussion with class and teacher, comment on materials used and how the task was tackled

Introduction

Problem-solving activities are excellent ways of introducing design and technology, or they may be integrated within long-term projects as mini-topics. Problem-solving activities have common features or phases that mirror, to some extent, the design process cycle:

- Imagining possible solutions to the problem (through 'brainstorming' and then recording all ideas generated)
- Selecting the most viable solution (taking account of limitations of time, materials, skills, etc)
- Acting to bring the selected solution to fruition
- Monitoring and evaluating the solution – fair testing against criteria for success.

Because problems are 'set', the first phase of the design cycle (AT1) *Identifying needs and opportunities* is often not covered by problem solving activities. Pupils nearly always start with *Generating designs* activities (AT2).

The key stage 1 Problem-solving topic is part of a larger topic on Toys. You can develop the activities under either heading. These examples should help you to identify problem-solving opportunities in all your topics. If you are running a topic on Toys for infants you can build in many opportunities for problem-solving activities. A topic on toys can include soft toys, construction toys, mechanical toys and inflatable toys. The problems that you can set should reflect this range. Here we offer three mini-topics that will in total take about six weeks to complete and that give good coverage of the pro-grammes of study for design and technology.

Getting started

Reception class children take time to settle in school. To help make children more relaxed it is a good idea to encourage your young children to bring their favourite toys to school (the toys may even stay overnight for a toys' party!) Such a process will also give you many openings for design and technology activities. Three activities are described below.

Resources and classroom organisation

By setting three different tasks to be accomplished over a period of six weeks you can divide your class into three groups and then sub-divide further into pairs of pupils. The advantage of this approach is obvious – you will not have to have unnecessary duplication of tools and equipment.

For the three tasks you will need to provide card of different thicknesses and colours, split pins, scissors, string, Sellotape, felt-tip pens, Fischertechnik, Lasy construction kits, plasticine (for weights), a wide variety of junk materials, paint, glues, double-sided tape and staplers, bulbs, wires and batteries.

Activities

To make a jointed teddy bear whose arms, legs and head can move This task will help your pupils to relate the movement of human limbs to those of the toy that they design and make. Children will make plans and then using split pins, glues and other methods of holding materials together construct their moving teddies. Your pupils may find that pushing split pins through card can be awkward and they may need help when trying to make the head move.

Your pupils will experiment, modify and persevere.

Use construction kits to make a moving see-saw model Children will explore how construction kit pieces fit together to make simple mechanisms. They will also be able to use weights to help operate the see-saw, thus introducing the concepts of balance and weighing.

Construct a junk model which can stand up on its own and that has a flashing light somewhere on its body This task should offer your pupils a variety of enjoyable activities. They will use materials in a creative way to make a robot-like model that can stand upright. Working with partners to decorate and wire up the robot involves a high degree of co-operation, discussion and problem solving.

Recording

Two-dimensional items can be stored in your pupils' folios. Models and other three-dimensional pieces of work may be worth photographing and annotating.

An example of recording

"Thomas quickly cut out the pieces for his teddy and assembled the legs and arms so that they moved freely by using split pins. Having studied the moving calendar Thomas was able to work out how to string up the limbs to make them move by pulling the string. He was one of the first children to devise a way of making the head move from side to side by adding a handle to the base of the neck, making a split at the top of the body to allow this movement."

Design and Technology Web – Problem solving KS 2

Identify needs and opportunities

- Teacher set problem

Evaluate

- The machine for testing the stretch of a piece of thread/string

Design and Technology Cycle

Generate designs

- For a machine for testing the stretch of a piece of thread/string

Plan and make

- A machine for testing the stretch of a piece of thread/string

National Curriculum coverage in design and technology

Design cycle phases

- **Identifying needs and opportunities** Provide oral justification for the conclusions they reach as a result of investigation
- **Generating designs** Very comprehensive coverage
- **Planning and making** Very comprehensive coverage
- **Evaluating** Very comprehensive coverage

The programme of study

- **Developing and using artefacts, systems and environments** Organise and plan their work carefully, introducing new ideas, so that their work improves. Allocate time and other resources effectively throughout the activity. Plan how practical activities may be organised. Identify the parts of a system and their functions and use this knowledge to inform their designing and making activities

- **Working with materials** Use equipment safely. Select materials for their task, rearrange materials to change their strength or character, and increase their usefulness. Join materials in semi-permanent forms, assemble materials. Finish work carefully

- **Developing and communicating ideas** Plan and structure their communication of ideas and proposals. Use drawings and plans to investigate and develop ideas for three-dimensional objects. Use modelling to explore design and technological ideas. Use modelling and recording when generating ideas. Break design tasks into subtasks and focus on each in turn as a way of developing ideas. Use materials and equipment to produce results which are aesthetically pleasing

- **Satisfying needs and addressing opportunities** Consider the possible consequences of their design proposals before taking them forward to completion, evaluate each stage of their work, make adjustments as a result of evaluation

---

Cross-curricular coverage

- **English** Pupil self-evaluation, planning and monitoring activities
- **Mathematics** Measuring, calculating, predicting, data presentation
- **Science** Gravity, weight, materials, structure

Introduction

This problem has been set within a larger topic on weight. Children are set the task of designing, making and evaluating a machine for testing the stretch qualities of lengths of string and other thread.

Getting started

Designing and making a machine for testing the stretching of pieces of string This problem has been used successfully as part of a topic on weight; you may find that it fits well within all of the following topics:

- Gravity
- Weight
- Structure
- Machines
- Materials
- Change.

As a background to setting the problem you should ask your pupils to consider that:

- Objects are pulled towards the earth
- Weight is a measure of how hard that pull is
- The strength of an object or structure depends on its shape and on the material from which it is made

- Different materials have different properties
- Materials are used for purposes for which their properties make them suitable.

Resources and classroom organisation

We recommend that this problem be used with classes of 9- or 10-year-olds working in groups. You will need to provide cardboard, wooden circles, cotton reels, rulers, yoghurt cartons, construction materials, Blu-tack, plasticine, hooks, scissors, pins, pens, Sellotape and glue.

As your pupils will be working through well defined phases and activities you will need to make sure that there is sufficient space for the planning and making activities for the whole class at a time – you may need to borrow more scissors when your pupils are working in rotating groups than you usually have available.

You should specify the types and amounts of materials that can be used, and set a time limit.

Activities

Having introduced concepts relevant to the problem ask your pupils to investigate the stretching properties of different samples of thread. Then ask them to design, make and test a machine to measure the stretch of a number of types of thread. The activities will include measuring, sticking, cutting and weighing.

Recording

Problem solving helps to structure recording activities. Firstly, your pupils will record their ideas. Secondly they will select, plan and make their chosen solution to the problem. Finally, they will test their products and evaluate the processes that they have been through. Your pupils should write up an account of what they do and make a thorough evaluation of their work. You will be able to annotate your pupils' records and file them for future assessment. You will be able to point to:

- Improvements in vocabulary, the quality of discussion and communications
- Successes and weaknesses of the machines designed by your pupils
- Whether or not your pupils realise the importance of fair testing.

Photography will be important for recording problem-solving activities.

Celebrations key stage 1

Design and Technology Web – Celebrations KS 1

Identify needs and opportunities

- Know that previous and present cultures have used D&T to solve familiar problems in different ways
- Hindu Diwali lamp and Christmas candle-holder

Evaluate

- Assess finished products against aesthetic and functional criteria

Design and Technology Cycle

Generate designs

- Explain thinking behind chosen approach

Plan and make

- Tests and final products based on the materials to hand and examples

---

National Curriculum coverage in design and technology

Design cycle phases

- **Identifying needs and opportunities** Work includes most areas at key stage 1 and also at key stage 2. Providing justifications for the conclusions reached, and knowing that people in the past and different cultures have used design and technology to solve familiar problems in different ways

- **Generating designs** Work at levels 1, 2, 3 and 4

- **Planning and making** Work at levels 1, 2 and 4

- **Evaluating** Work at levels 1, 2, 3 and 4

The programme of study

- **Developing and using artefacts, systems and environments**
- **Working with materials**
- **Developing and communicating ideas**
- **Satisfying needs and addressing opportunities** Extensive, covering many areas at this level

Cross-curricular coverage

- **English** Language developments may include the use of words such as stable, base, texture, wick, time, cylinder, flame and descriptions of smell
- **Information technology** Use of word processor to write review of activities
- **Mathematics** Weighing, calculations, estimation, shape – two-dimensional and three-dimensional. Patterns
- **Science** Light, colour, heat, sight. Change in state of materials through application of heat
- **History** History of lighting and power and multicultural elements
- **RE** Strong elements both of Christian and Hindu celebrations and symbolism

Introduction

Christmas and the Hindu festival of Diwali both use light as a potent symbol. Christ is portrayed as the light of the world and a series of Diwali lamps mark the path of the Hindu god from darkness back to the world of light. The topic offered here has a number of valuable multicultural aspects and can be linked to other topics such as light. The main activity will be the designing and making of a Diwali lamp and candle holders.

Getting Started

As part of a Celebrations topic in the autumn term, that will naturally include Christmas, you can also give attention to celebrations of other cultures. The Hindu festival of Diwali tends to vary year-to-year as it is determined by lunar months, not calendar months. At the time of writing Diwali fell in the autumn term.

As part of an historical examination of lighting children were asked:

- What was life like before electricity?
- What would it be like to be blind?
- How can we make light that is controlled and mobile?

The plan to make a candle holder tied into other celebrations gave opportunities to:

" Know that previous and present different cultures have used design and technology to solve familiar problems in different ways."

AT1

Resources and classroom organisation

Your children will work in pairs and individually. You will need to pay attention to safety aspects, as lighting and testing the lamps will be an important part of the evaluation process.

If you wish to follow this example then you will need to provide and use a good range of stimulus materials that include, where possible, books, photographs and artefacts. Wax, clay, plasticine, flour and salt, string, weighing machines and paint will all be needed.

Activities

The activities will include:

- Discussing the range of celebrations, understanding that different cultures make and use different artefacts to help them celebrate
- Investigating conditions in which clay dries
- Melting wax, observing it solidifying
- Investigating coloured lights, observing mixing of coloured lights
- Investigating the effect of the size of candle flames of various shapes
- Handling clay and plasticine
- Modelling and moulding shapes
- Designing and making Diwali lamps
- Taking account of aesthetic considerations
- Weighing
- Evaluating success and failure.

You will need to use pertinent questions as part of the preparation and management of the practical activities. By including the Diwali lamp and the making of candle holders as part of the topic you will have the advantage of introducing different materials and problems – for example, pupils would have to ensure that the candle holder is capable of holding a candle upright; this brings into play considerations such as length and weight.

Candle holders and Diwali lamps can be made from a variety of materials such as clay, plasticine and dough.

The skills involved will include designing, making, moulding and decorating.

Beyond this it should be a very satisfactory topic with all children succeeding in making a holder that will stand upright; they will understand more about the properties of materials and develop their critical faculties when judging the success of the end product: how fit is it for its purpose? You may well find that the first attempt will be functional but unattractive; ask your children if can they improve its appearance.

Because of the need to judge the appropriateness of materials it is likely that observational skills will be enhanced. This work should be organised in groups; during the planning, making and evaluation phases there will be many opportunities for discussion and co-operation.

Recording

You will need to record important aspects of the discussions that take place and will also collect written evidence of the pupils' investigation, design and evaluation activities. Individual accounts, as sampled below, when annotated, dated and filed are valuable:

'We used some clay. We had 100 grams of clay which we weighed. It felt like a squashy bun. It smelt like paint. We rolled and pressed it into a lamp. We used our thumbs and made a lip. After 10 days my Diwali lamp is dry, it is lighter than 100 grams. I painted it and made some patterns on it. It was not easy to paint. My candle is made of wax. I made it last term. It is white blue. It is a cylinder. My candle is 3 cms long. I have made a candleholder to keep my candle up straight.'

As the products will be rather small it would be possible to store them, although you should consider the need to make a photographic record of the processes involved in the work as well as the finished product.

Design and Technology Web – Celebrations KS 2

Identify needs and opportunities
- Need to produce musical instruments that are attractive for part of a carnival

Evaluate
- By attempting to play a piece of music
- Aesthetics of the finished design

Design and Technology Cycle

Generate designs
- For musical instruments
- For decorating the instruments

Plan and make
- Musical instruments with hollow and solid sounds that can be tuned and play a tune

---

National Curriculum coverage in design and technology

Design cycle phases

- **Identifying needs and opportunities** Start with unfamilar situations. Provide oral and written justification for the conclusion they reach. Know some ways people in different cultures and times dealt with similar problems.

- **Generating designs** Make design proposals, use designs and models, record how they have explored different ideas, record the progress of ideas, extend and change ideas

- **Planning and making** Choose resources, use hand tools, improvise, minimise waste, choose tools, use drawings, use knowledge of materials

- **Evaluating** Full range of evaluation activities, verbal and written

The programme of study

- **Developing and using artefacts, systems and environments** Identify what should be done and ways in which work should be organised

- **Working with materials** Explore and use a variety of materials to design and make things. Recognise that materials are processed in order to change or control their properties. Recognise that many materials are available and have different characteristics which make them appropriate for different tasks. Join materials and components in simple ways. Use materials and equipment safely. Select materials for the task. Assemble materials, finish work carefully

- **Developing and communicating ideas** Use imagination and their own experience to generate and explore ideas. Represent and develop ideas by drawings, models, talking, writing and working with materials. Find out, sort, store and present information for use in designing and making. Take account of other people's reactions to aesthetic characteristics. Use drawings and plans to investigate and develop ideas for three-dimensional objects. Use materials and equipment to produce results which are aesthetically pleasing

- **Satisfying needs and addressing opportunities** Evaluate their finished work against the original intention. Consider the needs and values of individuals and of groups, from a variety of backgrounds and cultures. Evaluate each stage of their work, make adjustments as a result of evaluation, use their appraisal of the work of others to help their own work

---

Cross-curricular coverage

- **English** Discussion, vocabulary extension. Written records of plans, progress and evaluation

- **Mathematics** Measurement, estimation, symmetry, shape, area, volume

- **Science** Vibration, pitch, sound and materials

Introduction

Many towns and cities have carnivals and civic celebrations. Some of these are linked with important annual ethnic events, while others appear to have no particular function. The variety of brilliant displays, costumes and musical extravaganzas offer you excellent points of departure for design and technology activities. This topic is designed for a class of eight- or nine-year-olds working in groups of three or four. It is a mini-topic (to last one or two days) on musical instruments set within the long-term topic of Carnival.

Getting started

Having seen the variety of musical instruments that are played during carnivals you can set your pupils the task of producing an unusual, attractive instrument which can be used to play a tune. The instrument can be of any type that can be constructed from the materials that are made available.

Resources and classroom organisation

Pupils should be organised into groups of three or four. You will need to provide information about carnivals, celebrations and musical instruments. Books about ancient, modern and multicultural instruments will be very useful. You may find that your local museum service can provide examples of musical instruments. If you have strong, well organised local communities from the Indian sub-continent, the West Indies and China you may well find that parents and friends can provide valuable resources for display. Also, it may be possible that local artists and musicians can be involved in your topic by giving demonstrations and helping to evaluate the finished instruments.

Cardboard boxes (shoe boxes), gourds, bottles, dowelling, string, nylon threads (of different thicknesses), glues, paints, cotton wool, scissors, elastic bands, yoghurt pots, cardboard, water and sand, hand tools (including junior hacksaws and drill), and rulers will be needed.

Activities

Designing and making When designing and making musical instruments, your pupils will develop their understanding that a system is made of related parts which, when combined, can achieve the goal of playing a tune.

They will have to organise and plan their work carefully, introducing new ideas so that when the sounds produced are not at the right pitch they can be changed to be in tune. Because the task is not heavily prescribed all the groups will be able to come up with their own individual designs.

Using materials Pupils will explore and use a variety of materials in their designing and making activities. They will probably find

difficulties in joining different materials and components in simple ways and will have to experiment with the right kinds of glues before finally fixing things in place. As part of the design brief is to produce an attractive instrument, the children will have to use materials and equipment in safe and aesthetically pleasing ways.

Investigating sound Your pupils will be involved in researching into how sound is produced and will have to consider:

- Sound from hollow objects
- Sound made by vibrating strings
- Whether or not length of string affects pitch
- What happens to pitch when they change the level of water in bottles
- Whether the tension of strings/elastic bands affects pitch.

They will have to use imagination, and their own experience, to generate and explore ideas in tackling the task that they have been set. As they are aware of the community aspect of their work they should develop an understanding that other people's reactions are important.

Evaluating Having a specific goal in mind, your pupils will be able to evaluate their finished work against the original intention easily by performing in front of the rest of the class. You could hold a class review to appraise the attractiveness of each other's work.

Recording

Plans, designs, evaluations and photographs of the musical instruments should be dated, annotated and filed.

Design and Technology Web – Transport KS 1

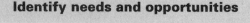

Identify needs and opportunities

Design and Technology Cycle

Evaluate
- Test buoyancy and ability to support weights
- Problem solving – experiment with different materials to see which will float and which will sink

Generate designs
- For models of bicycles, boats – draw from models and still life
- Use construction kits
- For a bus from construction kits and 'scrap materials'

Plan and make
- Lego cars
- A road for toy cars out of wooden bricks/blocks
- A garage the right size to take a Lego car
- Junk modelling of a car
- Lego model of trains
- Balsa model of car

National Curriculum coverage in design and technology

Design cycle phases

- **Identifying needs and opportunities** See how to change their work

- **Planning and making** Making simple things using a variety of materials. Describe to others how they are going about their work. Use knowledge of the characteristics of materials in making artefacts, systems and environments

- **Evaluating** Consider and describe what they have done with classmates and teacher

- **Designing** Make changes in design

The programme of study

- **Developing and using artefacts, systems and environments** A very full programme of work

- **Working with materials** Use, join and assemble materials

- **Developing and communicating ideas** Use imagination and represent ideas through visual and verbal means

- **Satisfying needs and addressing opportunities** Evaluate work against original intentions

Cross-curricular coverage

NB numbers refer to week numbers (see text on page 68)

- **English**
  1. Talking and writing about *Story of the Town,* Story Chest
  2. Talking and writing about cars. How they move, different kinds: racing, three-wheeled, open-top sports cars, etc
  3. Talking and writing about bicycles. Writing traffic survey forms, writing-up results, discussing different forms of transport on roads – lorries, cars, motor-bikes, buses
  4. 'One-eyed Jake'; talking and writing about boats and Pirates – learning the poem of 'One-eyed Jake'
  5. Talking about buses and planes
  6. Writing and talking about boats, different types – yachts, tugs, passenger liners, ferries. Writing and performing play based upon 'One-eyed Jake'
  7. **a)** Role play – going on bus journey on bus made this week
     b) Talking and writing about hot-air balloons.
  8. Story of Mr Gumpy's motor car
  9. Talking about and writing about steam trains; 'Thomas the Tank Engine'
  10. Writing about making wooden model of car
  11. Talking about journey of Jesus on a donkey

- **Mathematics**
  3. Traffic survey outside school. Drawing a picture of a bus and putting a person in each window. How many people altogether?
  4. Using and making balls of equal size, counting number of balls to make boat sink. Measuring materials to make boats.
  5. Putting a person in each plane window
  6. Making graphs using data collected in traffic survey
  7. Using money to buy bus tickets and receive change
  8. Making a class graph of car colours owned by parents
  10. Measuring balsa for car model toy cars/scooters

- **Science**
  3. Observation of mechanisms
  4. Moving position of balls – effect on stability

- **Art and design**
  1. Using paint and silver foil to make 'My Silver Jumping Stick' from story for wall display. Using felt pens for making pictures of car transporter

2. Drawings of houses and observational drawings of cars and models

3. Observational drawings of bicycle. Making a collage of different types of cars for display. Felt-tip observational drawing of monoplane

4. Colour mixing, making patterns. Making a collage of 'One-eyed Jake' using fabrics, buttons, sequins, etc. Observational drawings of toy boats

5. Painting picture of *The Big Red Bus*

6. Frieze of island scene of Jake and his pirate ship, observational drawing of a yacht (toy); junk modelling of garage for car

7. a) Making self-portraits while on school bus
   b) Making a painting of an air-balloon, suspend from ceiling

8. Making a large model of Mr Gumpy's car for use in drama using card and paint, helping make animal masks for Mr Gumpy's play. Using plasticine to make model

9. Observational drawing of Thomas the Tank Engine toy and model of Stephenson's Rocket

10. Decorating and finishing car model

Introduction

Introducing design and technology activities for very young children can be difficult. Transport is a familiar topic which can contain excellent design and technology activities. The topic opens with a storytelling, extends for the whole term and ends in work on Jesus' Easter journey on a donkey.

To give you a sense of sequence we have numbered the points according to the week within which the activities are planned to take place. The topic described below is not intended to be prescriptive. It is given to show how design and technology activities can be integrated within topics for even the youngest children as long as the basis of their work is in the form of structured play.

The design and technology activities will include:

- Week 1 Making Lego cars
- Week 2 Making a road for toy cars out of wooden bricks/blocks
- Week 3 Designing and making models of bicycles – drawing from models and still-life, using construction kits
- Week 5 Designing and making boats
- Week 6 Making a garage the right size to take a Lego car
- Week 7 Designing and making a bus from construction kits and 'scrap materials'
- Week 8 Junk modelling of a car
- Week 9 Lego modelling of trains
- Week 10 Making a balsa model of a car.

Getting started

In this outline of a topic on Transport we encourage you to see the many splendid opportunities that exist. The topic is planned to extend for the whole of a spring term.

Resources and classroom organisation

Your pupils will work in pairs, groups and as a class; they must have access to a good range of relevant books. Other resources should include construction kits such as Bauspiel, Lego and Fischertechnik, wooden blocks and bricks, scrap materials, balsa, glues, still life objects such as bicycles (full size or models) and moving mechanisms.

Paper, plasticine, fabrics, buttons, sequins, silver foil, card and paints will be included amongst other necessary materials.

Activities

Besides the range of activities given in the introduction above there are other opportunities for design and technology that will occur in the construction of models.

Model aeroplanes Following a discussion about aeroplanes initiated with questions such as:

- Have you ever flown?
- What was it like?
- What is the best shape for an aeroplane?

questions about symmetry will arise and lead to the practical problems of how to support the wings of model aeroplanes that could be hung from the ceiling. Here, additional skills and materials can be introduced. With adult help your pupils will be able to use small pea sticks and silver foil to strengthen and cover their card models.

Cars and ramps When working with toy cars that your pupils bring to school you may ask them to consider:

- How far can different cars travel?
- Do metal, wood or plastic perform well?
- Do the fastest cars necessarily travel the farthest?

By designing ramps of varying heights many experiments can be set up that will help answer the questions that you and your pupils will pose.

Ramps and bridges From the construction of ramps you can naturally progress and start to work with related structures such as bridges. Here are opportunities to add traffic signals and to discuss colours and the most appropriate placing of traffic lights to control the flow over the bridge. Such activities will involve valuable educational experiences:

- Discussion over placement of lights
- How to support the bridge
- Measuring of the signals, thinking of the best shapes and colours
- Considering what weight the bridge can support
- Drawing pictures of cars, bridges, houses and people to add reality to the scene.

The work on buses could be extended by examining old-fashioned bus tickets and ticket machines and following this up by designing new versions.

Recording

Selected pieces of work, annotated and dated, will suffice.

Sample of pupil's own recording

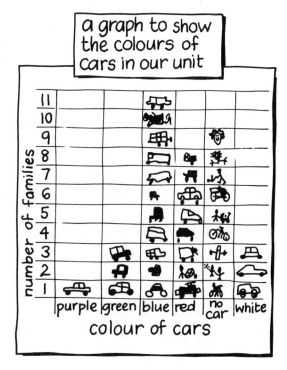

69

Transport key stage 2

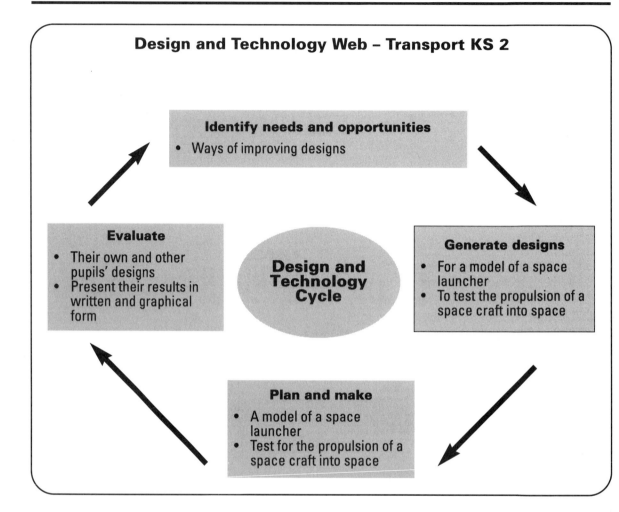

Design and Technology Web – Transport KS 2

Identify needs and opportunities
- Ways of improving designs

Evaluate
- Their own and other pupils' designs
- Present their results in written and graphical form

Design and Technology Cycle

Generate designs
- For a model of a space launcher
- To test the propulsion of a space craft into space

Plan and make
- A model of a space launcher
- Test for the propulsion of a space craft into space

National Curriculum coverage in design and technology

Design cycle phases

- **Identifying needs and opportunities** Provide oral and written justifications for the conclusions reached

- **Generating designs** Very comprehensive coverage in this area

- **Planning and making** Almost complete coverage of these processes at this key stage

- **Evaluating** Thorough evaluative processes required, with the exception of cultural diversities

The programme of study

- **Developing and using artefacts, systems and environments** The activities provide a comprehensive programme in this area, with the exception of the need to use a variety of information sources in developing proposals

- **Working with materials** Opportunities exist for a complete coverage of the use of materials, with the possible exception of the rearrangement of materials to change their strength or character

- **Developing and communicating ideas** Use of plans, diagrams and modelling

- **Satisfying needs and addressing opportunities** Limited coverage of this area

Cross-curricular coverage

- **English** Discussion and decision making, plan writing, evaluation preparation

- **Information technology** Word processsing. Data preparation and presentation

- **Mathematics** Estimating, measuring, comparative line graphs

- **Science** Energy, forces, weight, inertia. Consideration of materials' properties and characteristics

Introduction

This is a problem-solving activity, part of a long term topic on space transport. The problem is to design and make a mechanism that will launch a ping-pong ball at least a metre into the air.

In such problem-solving activities the first phase of the design cycle, *Identifying needs and opportunities,* is replaced by the teacher-set task. A strength of this problem is found in developing and using artefacts, systems and environments and working with materials.

Getting started

This is a mini-topic from within a term-long topic on Transport and is a problem-solving activity in which a teacher-set task replaces AT1. This mini-topic is particularly strong for

working within the programme of study PoS1, *Developing and using artefacts, systems and environments* and PoS2, *Working with materials.* Pupils are required to use their imagination to design, make and test their solutions to the problem.

The problem Design and make a mechanism that will launch a ping-pong ball at least a metre into the air. The source of energy should not be from blowing actions. The mechanism should be a model of a full-scale design for a space ship launcher. Pupils will need to propose a number of possible solutions, select the most viable design, make and then test the mechanism. Records of a series of three test 'firings' should be averaged and the results of each pair of pupils' work presented on a class bar chart.

Resources and classroom organisation

In this set problem, your children will work best in pairs, as this gives good opportunities for close co-operation and discussion of the details of possible solutions to the problem. Elastic bands, tubes, yoghurt pots, dowelling, ping-pong balls, corks, lolly sticks, Sellotape and scrap materials, glues and simple hand tools will be needed.

Activities

These include:

- Understanding the problem
- Controlled 'brainstorming' activities
- Recording of the ideas that are generated.

This initial creative phase is followed by reflective discussion amongst the pairs of children and the selection of the most appropriate solution to the problem. The specific limited range of materials, the time available and, of course, the set task should all be important considerations as they prepare their design proposals.

The practical activities will include designing and making, estimating, measuring, cutting, fixing, operating, recording, evaluating and modifying designs, fair testing and presenting results.

Recording

Your pupils will produce:

- Records of their ideas
- Designs and plans
- Mechanisms
- Results from fair testing
- Evaluations of the success/failures of their mechanisms.

The two-dimensional items can be accompanied by photographs of the mechanisms, annotated, dated and filed in the pupils' folios.

Examples of outcomes

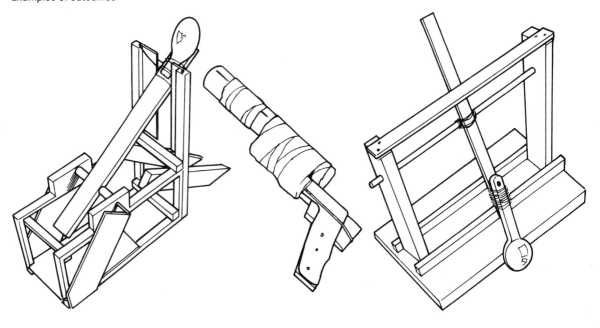

72

Design and Technology Web – Conservation KS 1

Identify needs and opportunities

- Pond environment in the classroom/school

Evaluate

- Frogs that jump
- Peep-hole environment
- Shadow puppets
- Fishing nets for different purposes

Design and Technology Cycle

Generate designs

- For frogs that jump
- For peep-hole environment
- For shadow puppets
- For fishing nets for different purposes

Plan and make

- Fishing nets (various materials, lengths, sizes of holes)
- Moving pond pictures
- Shadow puppets and music on underwater life

National Curriculum coverage in design and technology

Design cycle phases

- **Identifying needs and opportunities** This topic gives children at key stage 1 the chance to satisfy completely the first phase of the design cycle

- **Generating designs** This topic will give children a rich experiences of designing. In one instance the work will demand achievement at a high level – children will be required to estimate the resource requirements and check on availability

- **Planning and making** Virtually a comprehensive coverage at key stage 1 using drawings and diagrams to assist making, using knowledge and understanding of the properties of a range of materials in their planning and making

- **Evaluating** besides work at key stage 1 children will have experience at key stage 2 reviewing the decision-making processes used in producing final artefacts and justifying the ideas, materials and components used

The programme of study

- **Developing and using artefacts, systems and environments** Know that a system is made of related parts, identify the jobs done by the parts of a system. Learn to identify what should be done and ways of organising work
- **Working with materials** A comprehensive coverage at key stage 1 with additional work at key stage 2 using equipment safely, selecting materials for the task and joining materials in semi-permanent and permanent ways
- **Developing and communicating ideas** Use imagination and explore ideas, represent and develop ideas through drawings, plans and writing
- **Satisfying needs and addressing opportunities** Evaluate the finished work against original intentions

Cross-curricular coverage

- **English** Concertina of frog life cycle. Vocabulary – slimy, cool, jumping, dive, etc. Phonic work f, fl, fr. 'I am a frog', creative writing
- **Mathematics** Partitioning of sets – duck-pond; addition – frogs, fish, ducks
- **Cookery** Rock buns, biscuit shapes, designing an edible environment
- **Science** Water surface tension, care of creatures, care of environment, study of pond water, microscope, experiment on breathing out of and under water
- **Art and craft** Clay pond creatures, pleated fish, tadpoles, paper weaving, sewing shapes
- **RE/moral education** 'Frog and Toad Alone', friendship, caring, sharing the environment

Introduction

This topic about pond life, which is designed to last a whole term, can be introduced by storytelling or a visit to a pond. Subsequently your pupils will create their own pond or use an existing pond in the school. From this a range of activities can evolve. The design and technology activities can include:

- Designing and making (environments, food, moving toys)
- Working with materials
- Experiments (both scientific and technological)
- Problem solving
- Dance and theatre.

A topic such as conservation will clearly need to be developed in a variety of different ways with different age-groups. Here at key stage 1 it is focussed around the topic of pond life.

Getting started

Stories are the most natural way of starting or complementing topics for young children; this topic is no exception. Young children have a strong empathy with their toys and living creatures; the topic that we outline here stems from an interest in pond life.

This topic is planned to last a term, and includes a number of points of departure for mini-topics. It will allow your children opportunities both to observe first-hand and to use books, stories, pictures, charts and videos to find out about a variety of animal and plant life. With time, children can take responsibility for the care of living things, and maintain their welfare by understanding their needs and the degree of care required.

The topic is designed for reception class and first year infants and covers art, design and technology, science, mathematics, language, music, movement and RE/moral education. Your pupils will create their own pond or use an existing one. This will form the focus of a range of activities related to various forms of pond-life. The practical aspects of the work can involve the activities listed in the introduction to this topic.

Resources and classroom organisation

Because of the range of activities that can be undertaken it is a good idea to split your class into groups, perhaps giving them names such as Fish, Tadpoles, Frogs and Ducks. You will find that a large proportion of the time will be used to undertake practical activities, some evolving from stories and poems, songs and rhymes while other activities will be more task-orientated.

You can introduce the topic with stories, poems, songs and rhymes such as *Frog and Toad*, Aesop's fables, *Tiddalik*, *Daddy fell into the pond*, *The Frog Prince*, *Five Little Frogs Sitting on a Well*, *Five Little Speckled Frogs* and *Six Little Ducks*. You will need to provide a wide range of materials that will include nylon stockings, muslin, lace doilies, different fabrics, yoghurt pots, cardboard boxes, plastic sheet, dowelling, scissors, glue, paint, Sellotape and paper and card.

The Pond If you do not have a school pond then your children can help to create one specifically for this project. A child's swimming pool can be filled with pond water and plants and then located inside your school.

Activities

Designing and making We suggest four activities in this category as outlined below.

Fishing nets

Ask your children to choose various materials to make fishing nets that will catch specific creatures without harming them. The right kind of questions to ask is important, so that you structure the play activities without being over prescriptive: 'Would a net to catch frog spawn have to be different from a net to catch frogs, plant life, water beetles or other creatures?' Such questions will help emphasise equally both science and technology. Creative work may result in a theatrical performance involving composed music, and a class play on fish and plants.

A moving picture

Your children can design and make a pond picture where something happens or moves; in completing such tasks they will show that they are:

" *Able to make artefacts, systems and environments, prepare and work to a plan and identify, manage and use appropriate resources, including knowledge and processes.* "

AT3

A sub-aquatic environment

If your children make their own pond environments (constructed from shoe boxes and coloured acetate) they can arrange them to be 'peephole' dioramas of their own sub-aquatic worlds.

An underwater display

Food

It is easy to integrate food within the topic if you work with adult helpers. Your pupils can design and cook biscuits and rock buns derived from the natural forms of aquatic life.

Working with materials For certain tasks your pupils may select polythene in preference to normal netting materials (for the safe examination of spawn and baby frogs, for example). In doing so your pupils will show a degree of knowledge and understanding of the properties of materials and the way properties of materials determine their uses and form the basis for their classification.

In the testing of a variety of materials to see what will or will not pass through them a number of considerations to do with function are important. Nets may be useful for collecting small fish, but would they be helpful in the examination of developing tadpoles and frogs? Which would be best for each identified need: nylon stockings, muslin, lace doiley, different fabrics or yoghurt pots?

Children can then choose what they think will be the best material for making their various collecting tools/nets; they can then test them in the school pond.

Collecting and using data The various specimens found over a period of time in the pond can be counted and sorted and information from the collected data can then be presented in a series of bar charts.

Science and language Adopting this investigative approach can give children the opportunity to learn biological language. Pupils will develop their knowledge and understanding of the organisation of living things and of the processes which characterise their survival and reproduction. The metamorphosis from spawn to full-grown frog will allow many scientific concepts to be explored in detail. Also, the evolution of the frog from its spawn gives some good opportunities for development in the pupils' knowledge and understanding of variation, and its genetic and environmental causes, as well as the basic mechanisms of inheritance, selection and evolution.

Mathematics In the making of the nets it will be necessary to measure the length of the handle. Exercises to be undertaken can include addition: adding the number of frogs, ducks and fish. Prior to addition you can ask your pupils to estimate the number of creatures. Pupils will also be involved in ordering and partitioning sets and showing that they are able to recognise and use patterns, relationships and sequences.

Your pupils will use shape and space and handle data in practical tasks in real-life problems in the design and making of their own pond-models.

Movement Curling, stretching and jumping on apparatus can all be made to be part of this topic.

Music Various noises including those made by frogs, football rattles and sand blocks can be combined in a 'musical' form.

Games *Frog and fly* is a popular and appropriate game.

Recording

Each pupil should be asked to keep their own 'Pond books' in which they can record new words, experiments and drawings. These will offer excellent opportunities for recording/assessment and evaluation. Make sure to date all entries and annotate any work that you choose for the children's folio.

Testing nets

Design and Technology Web – Conservation KS 2

Identify needs and opportunities

Design and Technology Cycle

Evaluate
• Fair testing of boat

Generate designs
• For a mechanism to raise the *Mary Rose* and preserve it once raised
• For models

Plan and make
• Wind strength tester
• Scale model of *Mary Rose*
• Boat to support a given weight
• Make and use templates
• Dark box for experiments on light

National Curriculum coverage in design and technology

Design cycle phases

• **Identifying needs and opportunities** Complete coverage with exception of knowing that people in past and other cultures approach problems differently

• **Generating designs** A comprehensive coverage of this phase of the design cycle at key stage 2

• **Planning and making** Possible complete coverage of this at key stage 2

• **Evaluating** Complete coverage apart from multicultural aspects and economic awareness aspects

- **Information Technology** This topic offers exceptional coverage at key stages 1 and 2. Not covered are the need to question the accuracy of information stored on computers, reviewing their experience of information technology and considering applications in everyday life. Using IT to present information in different forms for specific purposes

The programme of study

- **Developing and using artefacts, systems and environments** Very full opportunities for these

- **Working with materials** Full range of opportunities

- **Developing and communicating ideas** Possible full coverage

- **Satisfying needs and addressing opportunities** Limited coverage

Cross-curricular coverage

- **English** Factual accounts, visual descriptions, poetry on wild life. Stories, e.g. *The Magic*

- **Information technology** Recording information, interpreting information, pie graphs, data bases. Programs – *Bees, Suburban Fox, Flowers of Crystal, Into the Unknown, Dragon Trail, Edward, Pendown*; also word processing

- **Mathematics** Graphs, e.g. time/weight, height/weight, area/time, area/volume, mapping and deciphering quadrant readings, frequencies and distributions, e.g. plants

- **Science** Identification and classification, line transects, exposed/sheltered area. Growth rates (time/weight), recording. Food chains, food webs; pond life, energy states, chlorophyl, minibeasts, parasites, sunlight, air water, seasonal change, weather – pollution, predictions, creating habitats (indoor and outdoor), growth – seeds, bulbs, corms; frogs, toads and newts

- **Art and design** Plaster casts, collage – use materials from area. Sketching from still life, drawing to scale, textures

- **Geography** Mapping, compass directions, co-ordinates, grasslands, drought changing landscapes, natural/man-made landscapes – cities, rural and coastal landscapes. Sea levels – ozone layers, effects of the elements. Rocks, soils and minerals

- **History** Farming – past/present, rare and common plants and animals, evolution. Man's influence on conservation area and environment

- **Music/drama** Woodwind instruments, simulation, sounds, animals, wind, water, etc – soundwaves

- **RE** Moses, signs and symbols

Introduction

This topic shows that it is not necessary to take an obviously technological starting point to design and technology activities; it approaches Conservation from a completely different angle from key stage 1. The specific activities include:

- Designing and making weather instruments
- Making a boat to support a given weight
- Making a water filter to produce clean drinking water from canal water.

There are many opportunities for working with information technology.

Getting started

The topic described extends the kind of approach shown in the previous topic. This example, building carefully upon previous experience, covers many curriculum areas and deals with a number of requirements for design and technology. Great scope exists for dealing with many requirements of AT5 for capability in information technology.

The topic is very comprehensive and is planned to take a term to complete.

Resources and classroom organisation

For the boat you will need specific amounts of balsa wood, one sheet of sugar paper per pupil, a range of glues, materials for water-proofing the paper – such as wax candles – hand tools, sandpaper for finishing work, paints and brushes.

For the water filter you will need cotton wool, filter paper, nylon mesh and other meshes, granulated carbon, bottles and containers, plastic tubing, litmus papers and water purifying tablets.

You may also include junk materials such as boxes, plastic bottles and pots, straws, nails, split pins, corks, polystyrene, ping-pong balls and plasticine.

Activities

As the three topics are, to some extent, separate mini-topics we have written them accordingly.

Designing and making weather instruments The task here is to design, make and test instruments to measure different aspects of weather conditions. These include thermometers, barometers, anemometers and rain gauges.

Thermometer and barometer activities will include:

- Designing/planning stages in making
- Selecting materials
- Making – measuring
- Calibrating
- Positioning and fixing on calibrated board
- Choosing colouring for water for ease of viewing the thermometer
- Testing.

It will be necessary for your pupils to understand the principles of expansion of water when heated when they tackle the calibration of the thermometer. Likewise for the barometer, it will be necessary for your pupils to understand the principles associated with air pressure. You may find that your pupils will plan well the detail of the major aspects of the work but may need to adjust the more minor details. This is valuable experience and needs to be recorded.

There are many ways that your pupils can tackle the task of designing and making a machine for measuring the speed of the wind (anemometer). When setting the task you will need to be fairly specific; for example, pupils will need to decide whether it should show only the strength of the wind, or the direction as well.

A simple solution to the problem of showing the strength of the wind can be to make a measure using balsa wood and yoghurt pots.

Activities include:

- Developing a range of ideas
- Selecting ideas
- Designing
- Making
- Fair testing.

If you include the making of a weather house, then more practical activities will be introduced:

- Linking the technology of a simple barometer with mechanisms for moving model people
- Discussion of the type and thickness of materials to be used in the construction of the house
- Fairly complex planning, involving the sequence of construction – trying to predict any snag, (for example the inside must be finished before the front is fixed)
- Deciding the relative sizes of the doorways and the lady and man – on pivots
- Careful measurement and alignment of wood to make the walls of the house
- Selection of appropriate materials (catgut) to provide change in length, to twist and swing lady and man backwards and forwards
- Arranging swivel platform, so that it swings freely
- Decorating house and people. Making it realistic, to resemble a Swiss chalet.

Making a boat to support a given weight If you use a central general idea of conservation then you can cover many areas that involve different skills and activities. For example, you may discuss problems associated with conserving different materials –

such as sodden wood as found in the *Mary Rose*. A number of possible design and technology activities present themselves at this point, such as:

- Make a boat to support a given weight
- Fair test the boat
- Design and make/use templates in the making of the boat
- Design and make a mechanism to raise the *Mary Rose*
- Design ways of preserving the *Mary Rose* once raised.

Your pupils will cover further National Curriculum areas if you set a particular task, such as:

- Design and make a boat from one sheet of paper or a selection of other materials
- Waterproof the paper to make the boat
- Make the boat to be capable of supporting 10 grams weight
- Find out what the maximum load is that the boat can carry without sinking
- Record your decisions, and present the results of your tests in graphic form.

Your teaching programme will be extended to consider:

- Which materials float best
- What shapes to use
- How to make the boat more stable (perhaps by weighing it down in different places)
- Water-proofing, testing for absorbency
- Drawing, measuring, cutting, joining, fixing, assembling, modifying and finishing
- fair testing, adding measured weights until the boat sinks.

Making a water filter to produce clean drinking water from canal water This activity derives from a real problem with a historical perspective. How did canal folk gather clean drinking water: from wells en route, from the canal or where? If they used canal water, how did they ensure that it was safe and good to drink?

Your pupils can collect samples of water from ponds or rivers and imagine ways that they may be cleaned.

Observational skills will be needed throughout this work. The initial examination of the condition of the water supply will involve looking for:

- Litter
- Water creatures (dipping with nets)
- Bubbles rising from the bottom
- Water weed
- Clarity of water
- Smell of the mud.

In the designing and making of the filter system a number of considerations will have to be made, not least of which are criteria for success. Your pupils may design simple or complex systems; they will devise methods of determining how much dirt has been removed from the samples and present this data in a graphic form.

It may be that a variety of materials and methods are used while a simple evaluation of the one that caught the dirt best will decide success or failure. In this element of the topic you have a close union of the methodology of science and its application through design and technology to producing practical solutions to real problems.

Recording

Use photographs, select and collect examples of pupils' work. These should be dated, annotated and filed in children's folios.

A boat to lift the Mary Rose

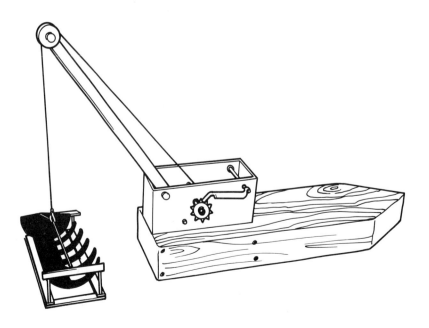

82

Wheels key stage 1

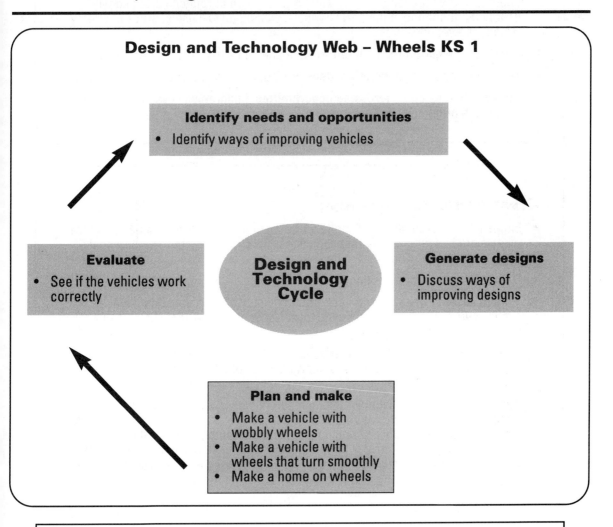

Design and Technology Web – Wheels KS 1

Identify needs and opportunities
- Identify ways of improving vehicles

Design and Technology Cycle

Evaluate
- See if the vehicles work correctly

Generate designs
- Discuss ways of improving designs

Plan and make
- Make a vehicle with wobbly wheels
- Make a vehicle with wheels that turn smoothly
- Make a home on wheels

National Curiculum coverage in design and technology

Design cycle phases

- **Identifying needs and opportunities** Will be identified in existing familiar artefacts. Children will describe what they find out in their explorations

- **Generating designs** Will involve verbal and pictorial expression about what may be done

- **Planning and making** Children will use a variety of materials to make simple things, they will describe what they are doing, use tools for cutting and shaping

- **Evaluating** Describe what has been done and how well. Children will discuss with teachers what they have done and how their work relates to the original task

The programme of study

- **Developing and using artefacts, systems and environments** Children will be taught to know that vehicles (systems) are made up of related parts and will identify the functions of the parts (wheels, axles) and will use sources of energy to make the vehicles move

- **Working with materials** Children will use and join a variety of materials

- **Developing and communicating ideas** By models and sketches

- **Satisfying needs and addressing opportunities** Children will evaluate their work against the original intention

Cross-curricular coverage

- **English** From 'brainstorming' make a display of new words in room. Find where wheels are in everyday life, fairgrounds, farms. Organise their own personal wheel books, choosing what to put in them. People who live in homes on wheels

- **Drama** Ways of moving, spinning, rolling, turning, stopping and starting

- **Art and design** Make a large background display of craft wheels on which to display survey work. Make spinning tops. Make collage wheels using pasta, string and junk mechanisms

- **Mathematics** Estimation, comparison, classification of variety of wheels on display. Timing – do they go fast or slow? Survey of wheeled vehicles outside school and wheeled articles at home. In class book sort wheels

- **Science** Collection of wheels. Taking mechanisms to pieces – old clocks and watches. Observing wheels on drills, food mixers, etc. Sand and water wheels. Making wheels move by pushing, pulling, and understanding that these forces can make things start moving, speed up, swerve and stop. Observing the tread of wheels (tyres), examining the materials used in tyres and the frame of wheels

Introduction

For very young children it is often easier to start design and technology activities by making simple artefacts or systems. The topic described below starts at this third phase of the design process cycle. Children are asked to make vehicles with certain specific characteristics which are then tested and modified. This topic is ideal for reception class children.

Getting started

This topic will introduce even the youngest children to a valuable range of activities. Similar topics have been used with great success with classes of 30 children aged four and five. It is planned to last for a term and is composed of a number of mini-topics carefully linked together.

Introducing the topic can be best achieved by asking questions such as: How could we cope without the wheel? Where do we find wheels? Why do we need them? In what ways do wheels move? Are there any special types of vehicles that don't use wheels, for example hovercraft and tanks? Are all wheels round? Do they need to be round?

For very young children it is a good idea to start as we do here with making activities.

Resources and classroom organisation

Your children will probably work in groups and by themselves. If you arrange for your pupils to make their own 'wheel book' their individual style and approach will be encouraged to develop.

There are many excellent stories, poems and songs about wheels. Books such as *Wheels* by Julie Fitzpatrick, *The Drive* by Helen Oxenbury, *Mr Gumpy's Motor Car/ Outing* by John Burningham, *Joe at the Fair* by Doreen Roberts and songs like, *The Wheels on the Bus* and *I Ride My Little Bicycle*.

You will need to provide sheets of card, cardboard boxes, cylinders, string, strong adhesive, paint, Lego or other infant level construction components, axles, cotton reels, wood and a choice of wheeled vehicles. Other useful resources include making a collection of many diferent kinds of wheels, filmstrips and videos and, if possible, visits to a farm or a waterwheel.

Activities

There are five main activities that we recommend as being particularly good. These are:

- Creating vehicles from junk and construction toys, with wheels that turn smoothly or run on wobbly wheels

- An activity involving building a sloping road to set instructions, choosing vehicles to run down the sloping road and monitoring and recording the findings on individual bar charts
- Turning your 'home corner' into a caravan (horse drawn)
- Creating a junk horse large enough to pull the caravan
- Finding a way of stopping a rolling cylinder at the bottom of a slope.

These activities will help your pupils to develop a range of skills and concepts besides those listed above. They include understanding that it is necessary to have smooth-turning wheels for vehicles, that the angle of slopes has something to do with the speed at which cylinders roll and that in following set instructions, working in co-operative groups there is often pleasure and efficiency. They will also have opportunities to explain and record their findings.

When considering their work on the horse-drawn caravan they will have the chance to understand something of the limited life-style of travellers – no electricity, no running water – while on the other hand they may think that it seems like great fun.

You may find that a topic such as this will allow girls to develop confidence in what they might otherwise consider to be 'boys' games'. In talking about their work and findings they will begin to develop the language upon which later progression will be based.

Recording

This can be easily managed by pupils having their own 'wheel books'. You can annotate, date and file these with their other practical work in their folios.

Wheels key stage 2

Design and Technology Web – Wheels KS 2

Identify needs and opportunities
- See how earlier civilisations solved similar problems
- Recognise ways of improving solutions to problems

Evaluate
- A 3D chariot with moving wheels based on 2D plans
- A wheel that will run down a slope in a straight line
- A wheel that will turn a corner as it runs down a slope

Design and Technology Cycle

Generate designs
- For a 3D chariot with moving wheels
- For a wheel that will run down a slope in a straight line
- For a wheel that will turn a corner as it runs down a slope

Plan and make
- A 3D chariot with moving wheels, based on 2D plans
- A wheel that will run down a slope in a straight line
- A wheel that will turn a corner as it runs down a slope

National Curriculum coverage in design and technology

Design cycle phases

- **Identifying needs and opportunities** Children will empathise with the problems of previous cultures

- **Generating designs** Children will have excellent design opportunities, making proposals, applying knowledge and skills, using models and sketches, seeking out and using information

- **Planning and making** Children will need to take account of the limitations of time and resources, work with others and use drawings, diagrams and models to assist making

- **Evaluating** The nature of the tasks will of necessity require review sessions with classmates and teachers; evaluation will be a continuous process

The programme of study

- **Developing and using artefacts, systems and environments** Pupils will be taught to organise their work and identify the parts of a system and their functions
- **Working with materials** Children will work with materials in a comprehensive programme set at their level
- **Developing and communicating ideas** Children will use drawings and plans to investigate and develop ideas for three-dimensional objects
- **Satisfying needs and addressing opportunities** Children will be taught that human shape, scale, proportion and movement affect the forms of design

Cross-curricular coverage

- **English** Working with a partner, discussing problems using language to probe possible solutions
- **Mathematics** Wheels will be of specified size; this will require the use of compasses; also the relationship between circumference and diameter will need to be considered. The chariot requires measuring and cutting and the making of curved shapes from straight pieces of card by attaching tabs

Introduction

Based within a wider topic on the Romans, this mini-topic on wheels provides a number of challenges. The tasks are strongly teacher-directed and as a result children will have limited scope for identifying needs and opportunities.

The first task, which will take a few days, is to undertake research and then make a two-dimensional design for a chariot. Following this stage children will use a variety of materials to make up a three-dimensional working model of a chariot that is based closely upon their plans.

The other two tasks are more directed and considered to be 'set-problems'. They are to design and make a wheel to run straight down a slope, and to design and make a wheel to turn a corner while rolling down a slope.

Getting started

The three activities build upon previous experience and originate in history; the starting point being the investigation of the development of chariots.

In the first task (to research and then make a two-dimensional design for a chariot), you should stress the importance of the function of a chariot – that of carrying a human being safely under conditions of danger. The need for mobility and ergonomically designed use of space is crucial. Children should study human proportions, read, plan and make designs. These models should then be scaled up and made from paper. Finally, having completed these stages, your pupils can make a three-dimensional chariot with moving wheels that is based upon their two-dimensional designs.

The other two specific tasks are to design and make a wheel to run straight down a slope and another wheel to turn a corner while rolling down a slope. These are intended to be completed in one session of two hours with a limited range of materials available.

Resources and classroom organisation

Children will work best in pairs with regular opportunities for reviewing the work of others in the class. A range of appropriate books that include historical and model-making information will be useful. Thin and thick white card, lolly sticks, axles, cotton reels, rods, wood (balsa), glues, artstraws, hole punchers and scissors will be needed.

Activities

Design and make a three-dimensional chariot with moving wheels, based on two-dimensional plans. After considering how Romans and Ancient Britons made chariots your pupils can draw together information and make their own designs. It is important to go through the prototype stage using paper before making the chariot with moving wheels. Your pupils will be involved in discussing the meaning of diagrams and plans. In particular they will have to consider what a bird's-eye view is, and how to describe side elevation and front views. This transformation of two-dimensional into three-dimensional should be an exciting process. They will be involved in making curved shapes out of straight pieces of card. They will also learn about the points listed opposite.

- Fixing axles and wheels
- Achieving balance
- Mobility
- Methods of sticking different surfaces.

Design, make and test a wheel that will run down a slope in a straight line and another one that will turn a corner. In this task children will be involved in:

- Realising that the position of the axles in relation to the wheel is important for smooth, straight running
- Discussing other designs with a partner or the class
- Testing designs, noting results
- Realising that accuracy in cutting circles is vital.

Recording

These types of activities lend themselves to comprehensive recording. Your pupils should keep a brief log of their activities. Such a log would include details of what they did, why they did it, the problems encountered and the fair test involved:

Model for a pupil log

Meanwhile you can observe and record any significant moments either in written form or as photographs.

Design and Technology Web – Structures KS 1

Identify needs and opportunities

- Understand the need to move stones
- Realise that water can carry great weights
- Understand that working together makes large projects viable

Evaluate

- Present day earth-moving equipment
- System for lifting stones
- Equipment for transporting stones

Design and Technology Cycle

Generate designs

- For system for lifting stones (15 kilos max)
- For equipment for transporting stones

Plan and make

- System for lifting stones
- Rafts, sledges, cylinders and ramps
- Platforms

National Curriculum coverage in design and technology

Design cycle phases

- **Identifying needs and opportunities** Seeing the need to transport heavy and awkward loads; empathising with earlier solutions to needs and opportunities. The context is historical, set in the school environment

- **Generating designs** Systems for lifting and moving stones through design proposals

- **Planning and making** Systems for lifting and moving stones

- **Evaluating** Success of previous cultures and children's own solutions to problems

The programme of study

- **Developing and using artefacts, systems and environments** Pulley systems, floating bridges, rafts, ramps – modifying pond banks to load raft

- **Working with materials** Junk bottles, clay, rope, pulleys, stone, water, construction kits

- **Developing and communicating ideas** Through drama on the Ancient Britons and Vikings (also through art), discussion, writing, drawing plans and diagrams

- **Satisfying needs and addressing opportunities** Problems solved in appropriate and efficient ways

Cross-curricular coverage

- **English** In writing about the way the Ancient Britons tackled the onerous tasks, the children will have to search for appropriate expression. In a similar way through drama activities new areas of experience will forge new forms of expression. Vocabulary extension

- **Art and craft** Making drawings and paintings of the Ancient Britons at work, carving 'early' sculptures, making jewellery

- **Mathematics** Using number. Measuring in practical tasks in real-life problems. Number operations, estimating. Recognising and using patterns. Appreciating the approximate nature of measurement. Using shape and space in real-life problems. Collecting, recording, processing, representing and interpreting data, estimating probabilities

- **Science** Planning, hypothesis and predicting; designing and carrying out investigations. Interpreting results and findings; drawing inferences and communicating results. The impact of human activities upon the Earth. Forces, gravity, energy (transfer and control), levers. Materials – sorting different stone types

Introduction

This imaginative, historically based topic with a special emphasis on engineering, covers many curricular areas. Children are faced with problems that were previously encountered by their forebears who constructed Stonehenge and other early structures. This topic has been used very successfully with classes of seven-year-olds who tried to find answers to a number of questions:

- What was the purpose of constructing Stonehenge?

- How was it possible to move and erect heavy stones?
- Why were the stones moved?
- What methods could the Ancient Britons use?

In finding answers to these questions, role play, drama and art and craft can provide vital avenues to children's imaginations. The children were set two specific tasks:

- Raise a stone (15 kilos) to a height of 2 or 3 metres
- Safely transport the stone over water for a distance of at least 4 metres.

This union of history and technology offers an exciting range of problem-solving processes and experiments that can be worked through in designs, plans, drawings, writings and models. This topic approaches Structures by looking at one famous structure: Stonehenge.

Getting started

The UK is rich in archaeological sites with many stone circles and earthworks – any of which may be a suitable starting point for the topic, should you wish to plan a visit. Outside the UK, the ancient civilisations of Egypt, Greece, Rome, the Incas and the Aztecs are also full of exciting design and technology learning opportunities.

Stonehenge is a familiar landmark on Salisbury Plain and for a group of seven-year-olds from a school in Melksham it was a source of inspiration for their project on stones. The children were very quick to put themselves in the position of the Ancient Britons and, stimulated by the mysterious spectacle of Stonehenge, their natural curiosity helped to provoke questions and eventually solutions to the problems faced by the original architects and builders.

You may introduce work on stone circles directly as an historical theme or as a natural progression from a more general topic on stones, gems and fossils.

Resources and classroom organisation

Drama activities will be likely to include the whole class.

The problems of finding ways to move large stones are best tackled as group activities. Obviously safety is a prime consideration, as children will be required to lift a stone weighing 15 kilos a height of 2 or 3 metres and thereafter transport the stone safely and under control across a pond over a minimum distance of 4 metres. If each group uses the same stone in turn then your organisational problems will be reduced.

The materials and resources that will be needed include a stone of known weight (you should know it, the children should find it out), lengths of fine strong rope with a minimum breaking strain of 30 kilos, pulleys and pulley blocks. Junk materials, including plastic bottles, logs (small), twine, strings and polythene bags (to simulate inflated animal skins) will be needed. You will also need graphic materials, paper and modelling cards, glues, a camera and film (for recording) and weighing scale and weights.

Activities

The activities will be linked to the two main tasks.

Lifting a 15 kilo stone a specific height For this task, children will be involved in imagining how the Ancient Britons raised the lintel stones to the top of the vertical stones. As part of this imaginative activity children will draw plans, write accounts of what happened and perhaps design and make clothes that the ancient workers may have worn.

Using pulleys and levers effectively will demand that children are able to carry out a range of mathematical calculations based upon the weight of the stone. Each group should make its own estimate and measurement of the weight of the stone, recording it carefully. Before groups attempt to raise the stone you will need to ensure that fixings are safe. By trial and adjustment methods, each group may discover:

- That using two pulleys can make the work a lot easier than one alone
- That two or three pulling on the rope makes work easier than if left to one

- That the time taken to experiment with pulley systems may save time in the end
- That the position of the pivot point (fulcrum) is important for the effective use of levers.

Transporting the stone across a pond of at least 4 metres width When tackling this task children will be faced with the prospect of using modern materials in place of those used by their forebears and will have to consider whether it is acceptable to use plastic bottles and inflated polythene bags in place of inflated animal skins as parts of rafts or floating bridges.

In designing and making methods of transporting the stone across the pond children will be involved in:

- Estimating the required size of the raft to support 15 kilos
- Calculations
- Selecting materials
- Joining materials together
- Making a system of control for the raft
- Fixing the stone to the raft.

- Finding a way of transporting the stone to the side of the pond

As there are many possible solutions to the problems, the teacher has a vital role of asking questions to stimulate thought and ideas, rather than providing answers and stifling imagination. Encourage children to make models of their suggested solutions as a means both of testing their proposals and communicating their ideas to their classmates. Pupils will be able to evaluate their own and other people's ideas in the light of alternatives and in terms of their response to the original task.

It is worth remembering that stone circles are sited in mystical or religious places and that the religion of the Druids could form another aspect for work on Stonehenge.

Recording

You will need to use photography to record the children's work as it progresses. This topic should produce some interesting plans and written accounts that can be placed in the children's folios.

Using a pulley to raise a stone

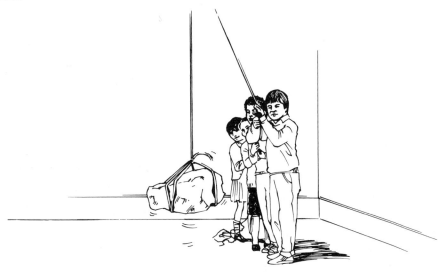

Structures key stage 2

Design and Technology Web – Structures KS 2

Identify needs and opportunities

- Set problem – make a tower at least 15 cm high (from paper provided) to support a weight of 1 kilo
- See ways of making weak materials into strong structures

Design and Technology Cycle

Evaluate

- Towers to support the given weight
- Strong and weak shapes

Generate designs

- For towers to support the given weight
- For strong and weak shapes

Plan and make

- Towers to support the given weight
- Strong and weak shapes

National Curriculum coverage in design and technology

Design cycle phases

- **Identifying needs and opportunities** By thoroughly investigating the potential of sheets of paper, opportunities for maximising the strength of weak materials may be realised

- **Generating designs** A variety of structures from a single sheet of paper. Designing strong and weak shapes

- **Planning and making** A variety of structures from a single sheet of paper. Designing strong and weak shapes

- **Evaluating** Not just a matter of whether the designs are successful or not: fair tests have to be established and used consistently. Testing the towers to destruction is a useful extension to the problem – some towers may be able to support 2, 3 or 4 kilos; what differences in design can account for the extra strength?

The programme of study

- **Developing and using artefacts, systems and environments** In designing strong and weak shapes pupils may well construct triangular and square shapes that can be considered to be systems
- **Working with materials** Very limited. Card, paper and paper studs and clips may be supplemented by glues
- **Developing and communicating ideas** Mostly through discussion with class-mates

Cross-curricular coverage

- **English** Discussion and criticism of each other's attempts. Writing about strong and weak shapes. Commenting on their own work
- **Mathematics** Measuring, calculation, estimation, shapes and space
- **Science** Materials, structures, forces, gravity and levers

Introduction

This is a mini-topic set within the wider context of a project on Buildings, Bridges and Towers. Technological activities include the use of different materials, shaping and joining them and making models of towers, bridges, girders and houses. In this topic children are set two specific tasks:

- Design and make a tower using one piece of paper that will support a weight of 1 kilo at a height of at least 15 cm above the surface of a table
- Using strips of thick card, paper clips and paper studs design and make strong and weak shapes. Use further strips of card to strengthen the weak shapes.

Getting started

The wider topic within which the tasks are set has considerable cross-curricular range. The scope includes:

- Making building materials (bricks with and without straw)
- Waterproofing materials for construction purposes
- The effect of weather upon buildings and structures
- Angles, area, measurement and tesselations
- History of bridge builders and architecture
- Rubbings of bricks, patchworks of houses
- Collage work on girders
- Models of bridges and houses.

The best time to set the two problems will depend on when you judge that the children have enough experience on which to draw.

Resources and classroom organisation

Make displays that include pictures of famous structures around the world, building materials, images of microscopic structures (the Van Nostrand Reinhold Visual Pack on structures is excellent) and plenty of books to do with buildings and structures. Try to arrange visits to new shopping centres, arcades and local areas that show the use of different building materials. Don't forget to take a camera with you.

You will need paper, card, scissors, glue, Sellotape, paper studs and paper clips, pencils and a number of 1 kilo weights.

Activities

Design and make a tower using a single piece of paper that will support a weight of 1 kilo at a height of at least 15 cm above the surface of a table. Children will discuss, cut, fold, assemble, fix and test their supports. Here are opportunities to explore what a fair test is. Encourage children to add progressively to the loads on their towers, (perhaps in 100 gram weights). Ask them to keep notes about what happens to the towers as the loads are increased until the point of collapse.

Design and make strong and weak shapes using strips of thick card, paper clips and paper studs. Use further strips of card to strengthen the weak shapes. Encourage the use of triangles, squares, rectangles and polygons which can then be strengthened by the use of struts. Children should make notes on their work and how they come to judge the strength or weakness of shapes. They should write a brief review of their findings.

Recording

Photographs of the making and loading of towers would provide useful evidence for assessment (you do not need to record every child). The flat shapes and written evidence should be annotated and filed.

A paper tower

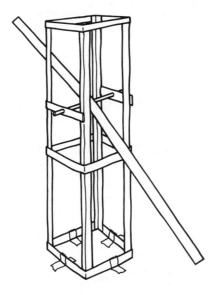

Food key stage 1

Design and Technology Web – Food KS 1

Identify needs and opportunities

- The visit of a beekeeper as a stimulus to baking a honey cake
- Mrs Wobble needs a box for her hamburgers
- The shopkeeper needs a container for sugar
- Dad needs a spoon rest for the kitchen

Design and Technology Cycle

Evaluate

- A honey cake
- A box for a hamburger
- A container for sugar
- A spoon rest

Generate designs

- For a honey cake
- For a box for a hamburger
- For a container for sugar

Plan and make

- A honey cake
- A box for a hamburger
- A container for sugar
- A spoon rest

National Curriculum coverage in design and technology

Design cycle phases

- **Identifying needs and opportunities** Realising that the supply of honey could be made into cakes. Imagining that Mrs Wobble needs a hamburger box and that Dad could use a spoon rest

- **Generating designs** The shape of the cake, a functional and attractive box and container for sugar

- **Planning and making** All of the above, plus the spoon rest which will most likely be made directly without any design element

- **Evaluating** Tasting, trying and discussing

The programme of study

- **Developing and using artefacts, systems and environments** Boxes and packages may be systems or artefacts

- **Working with materials** Clay, card, paper, foodstuffs

- **Developing and communicating ideas** In making the box for a hamburger children will have the opportunity to use graphical communication. Through evaluation children will be able to communicate ideas

- **Satisfying needs and addressing opportunities** This topic gives adequate coverage for infants

Cross-curricular coverage

- **English** Many opportunities for language development, for example from books and stories (see below for book list). New words may include creaming, folding, scoring, greaseproof, shining paper (foil), take-away, insulate and so on

- **Mathematics** Weighing, measuring, estimating, shapes (two- and three-dimensional), making corners

- **Science** Hot and cold, changes in state, energy, mixing materials, glazing and fixing clay with slip, melting of solids for cakes and cooking to make solid again as part of mixture

- **Art** Decoration and shaping

Introduction

Adequate provision must be made for building experience in home economics for boys and girls. Experience should include work on food and cookery. At a young age children will find that stories, visits to shops, farms and mills and, of course, their experiences in the home may provide good springboards for activities in this area of design and technology. The topic described for infants is cross-curricular and has been designed around stimuli from stories and a visit from a local beekeeper.

Getting Started

On page 98 is a list of mainly fiction books that will be useful as a way of starting work on food. Some will be more suitable than others for very young children, while all of them are suitable either for infant or junior levels. Inviting interesting people, such as a beekeeper, to school will provide a focus of attention.

In this topic we have put forward such a visit as one of the elements of an interesting programme of activities. The objectives of the topic should include the development of children's knowledge about healthy eating habits. You may also wish to start considering the environmental impacts of food production and touch upon the variety of foods that are available in the UK from our rich mixture of cultures. Cooking together in groups will develop social skills and help young children get to know each other.

Resources and classroom organisation

Food offers many opportunities for exciting classroom displays. Try to change these as the topic progresses and according to children's interests. Children can work by themselves, in pairs and in groups depending upon the activities.

Make available a good range of fiction and simple non-fiction books about food, our bodies, farming and so on.

Activities

Listening to stories will be followed by discussion that can be directed to consider a number of issues such as:

- How ancient people sweetened food and drink
- Why bees collect nectar
- How cakes are made
- What sort of package would be suitable to hold beefburgers
- What sorts of foods we need to keep healthy
- What junk food is
- How beefburgers are made (a simple food chain)
- How many kitchen utensils are needed in the home.

When cooking, children will be involved in working from recipes, measuring, estimating, creaming, baking and tasting.

When designing and making containers children will:

- Measure
- Estimate
- Fold
- Score
- Stick
- Cut
- Make
- Test
- Decorate.

Recording

This topic would lend itself very well to being recorded in a small 'food book' for each child. The book can then be a very useful basis for further work.

Suggested book list (some for infants, some for junior)

I Can Smell and Taste Peter Curry (Picture Lions)	*The Magic Pasta Pot* Tomie de Paola (Beaver books)
Eat Drink and Grow Susan Baker (MacDonald)	*The Enormous Turnip* Helen Oxenbury (Picture Lions)
Taste and Smell Doug Kincaid and Peter Coles (Nelson)	*Meg's Veg* Helen Nicholl and Jan Pienkowski (Puffin)
Kimi and the Watermelon Miriam Smith (Cape)	*Mrs Wobble the Waitress* Allan and Janet Ahlberg (Puffin)
The Avocado Pear Baby John Burningham (Cape)	
The Lighthouse Keeper's Lunch Ronda Armitage (Oliver and Boyd)	*The Ghost and the Sausage* Story Chest (Nelson)
The Tiger Who Came to Tea Judith Kerr (Collins)	*How do I Eat it?* Shigeo Watanabe (Bodley Head)
The Giant Jam Sandwich John Vernon Lord (Cape)	*Potato Man* Polly Pinder (Black)
Mr Greedy Roger Hargreaves (The Mill Trading)	*Dinner at Alberta's* Russell Hoban (Cape)
Little Miss Thin Roger Hargreaves (The Mill Trading)	*The Big Egg* William Mayne (Hamish Hamilton)
Maisie Middleton Nita Sowter (Lions)	*The Little Red Hen* William Stobbs (OUP)
The Gingerbread Boy Paul Galdone (Heinemann)	*Gregory the Terrible Eater* Mitchell Sharmat (Hippo)
Hansel and Gretel Jacob Grimm (Hamilton)	*James and the Giant Peach* Roald Dahl (Puffin)

Food key stage 2

Design and Technology Web – Food KS 2

Identify needs and opportunities

- Packages need to be attractive
- Different utensils have different functions
- Sometimes hand-operated machines are preferred to electrically powered ones
- Sometimes food needs to be preserved
- Sometimes food has to be processed

Evaluate

- Packages for food
- A hand whisk
- A milk cooler
- A windmill

Design and Technology Cycle

Generate designs

- For packages for food
- For a hand whisk
- For a milk cooler
- For a windmill

Plan and make

- Packages for food
- A hand whisk
- A milk cooler
- A windmill
- A chart showing root and leaf vegetables
- A block graph of food preferences

National Curriculum coverage in design and technology

Design cycle phases

- **Identifying needs and opportunities** Children will see that we need food for survival and that there are many opportunities for growing, processing, preserving and preparing food. Because of the need to distribute food long distances, packaging needs to be robust, and in order to attract sales packaging must be commercially effective and made from suitable materials

- **Generating designs** Milk cooler, hand whisk, packaging for new food product, a fair test for fat content, a working mill

- **Planning and making** Milk cooler, hand whisk, packaging for new food product and a working mill, charts and graphs

- **Evaluating** A continuous process

The programme of study

- **Developing and using artefacts, systems and environments** In this topic it is possible to develop and make artefacts, systems and environments

- **Working with materials** Card, paper, graphic material, plastics, foodstuffs, compost, seeds

- **Developing and communicating ideas** Through discussion, writing, drawing and the making of charts, graphs

- **Satisfying needs and addressing opportunities** Good coverage

Cross-curricular coverage

- **English** Discussion, gathering opinions from fellow pupils about their favourite foods, writing about growing seeds, development of reference skills

- **Information technology** Using data-handling packages for producing graphs about food preferences, word processing

- **Mathematics** Number work (mental arithmetic games): 'Yesterday I bought six oranges. I ate one and gave one to my friend. How many have I left?' Extensions to these plus subtraction and basic multiplication where appropriate. Weighing, money (visits to greengrocers to buy food), measuring, time (mealtimes and time for cooking/growing). Graph work on class food preferences

- **Science** Heat, cold, changes in state, bacteria, moulds, (using microscopes) – medicines from plants (rain forests) and moulds (penicillin). Edible and inedible plants, growing seeds (mung beans in the dark and in the light) classifying foods such as vegetables and fruit

Introduction

This topic follows on very well from the previous one, extending and enriching previous experiences. As the children are now at a more advanced level the work is more demanding. The range of activities includes the following sub-topics:

- Changes in food through heat and cold
- Packaging of food
- Preserving food
- Different kinds of food
- Cooked and uncooked food
- Energy
- Cooking equipment and utensils
- Constituents of food (vitamins, carbohydrates, protein, minerals, fibre, fats)
- Growing food
- Processing food – watermills and windmills
- Senses – smell, taste, sight.

Getting started

This topic may well develop from a harvest celebration (or reach its conclusion in such a festival). Alternatively it could originate from a study of Ourselves or, as with younger children, from stories and books. The aims of such a topic should include:

- Extending children's awareness of certain types of food which may encourage them to select for themselves more healthy foods than before

- Extending children's scientific understanding of concepts associated with food
- Understanding that people from different times and cultures have dealt with the need for food in different ways from our society (consider why convenience foods have been developed).

Resources and classroom organisation

It is essential to make the most of display opportunities; these will include:

- The great variety of foods, such as vegetables, fruit, breads, flours, meats and fish
- The ethnic richness available in the UK – Chinese, Indian, Italian, West Indian, Balinese, Greek and Mexican, for example
- Foods in different forms, solids to liquid: strawberry jam, jelly, puree, eggs – hard boiled to scrambled, and so on
- Ways of preserving food
- Varieties of spices (and other foods that can be identified by smell)
- Food left to show changes, i.e. mould, bacteria
- Cooking utensils for measuring, mixing, whisking, sieving, baking and serving
- The different ways food is packaged and labelled
- A collection of things that keep foods hot or cold (tea cosies, cups, vacuum flasks, newspapers, take-away dishes)
- Different forms of processing food – windmills, watermills, food processors.

Activities

Through discussion and using the displays of different food items, consider the nutritional content of different foods, such as vitamins, carbohydrates, fats and proteins, and how these are useful to our bodies. Look at how we store energy and how we keep warm. These activities will require children to communicate and interpret information.

As an extension of the first activity children can design and undertake tests on foods for fats. You may be able to raise the question of what will constitute a 'fair test'.

Making a limited number of food dishes will help show children that specific dishes can be nutritionally beneficial, such as fruit salad for vitamin C, carrot and potato soup for vitamin A, blackberry and apple pie (using wholemeal flour) for vitamin C and fibre.

Investigating different foods (flour, bread, root vegetables, fruits, nuts, eggs, fish, meat, beans and pulses) by scooping out, pulling apart, cutting cross-sections and drawing and writing about them will involve children in using magnifying glasses and microscopes and all five senses, noting similarities and differences. They will manipulate, measure, compare, classify, predict and communicate.

Children can observe how different families of food grow, and understand simple food chains. Children can grow food for themselves and use books for reference. Through these activities it is possible to gain a greater understanding of the inter-dependence of living and non-living things. They also help to highlight the relationship between inappropriate technology and damage to our environment, and how the right kind of technology can help us to solve global food problems. It is worth considering the conditions under which good quality food is best produced.

Activities that focus upon changes in food will include:

- Heating, cooling, freezing, dissolving and leaving food open to the air over a period of time
- Comparing freshly toasted bread with some that has cooled (weigh the same piece before and after)
- Comparing raw eggs with boiled, poached and scrambled ones (make meringues

with different amounts of sugar and at different temperatures).

Investigating the types of utensils used to handle food in its different forms can lead to interesting classification of materials such as wood, plastics and metal into groups according to function, .

Using construction kits children can design and make hand whisks.

Preserving foods will involve questions about why some foods keep better than others. Simple activities and tests can be carried out with fresh and sour milk, storing milk in different places (cool, warm, hot, covered, uncovered). Children can design utensils for storing milk and draw up specifications for the best storage conditions. Similar activities can be used for bread – does brown bread keep longer than white? Storing apples, peeled, and unpeeled, in lemon juice, or covered in cling film, will also provide information that could lead to technological activities of designing and making.

Games about recognising food through its smell (using feely bags) will challenge children's senses and help their powers of reasoning and communication.

Visits to farms (to see goats and cows being milked), supermarkets and corner shops should prove stimulating.

Designing and making models of windmills may be something of an old chestnut; nevertheless children are challenged on a number of fronts by such a task. Challenges are enhanced if you include specific requirements in the problem, such as making a device to raise a miniature sack of flour and lower it to the ground safely and under control.

Recording

Written work, drawings, graphs and photographs of stages in the production of models should be selected, annotated, dated and kept in children's folios.

Investigating food

102

The post key stage 1

Design and Technology Web – The post KS 1

Identify needs and opportunities
- The need for protective packaging for a delicate object
- The need for an envelope for a special purpose

Evaluate
- Fair test packages and envelopes

Design and Technology Cycle

Generate designs
- Express ideas about how to satisfy needs

Plan and make
- Use a variety of materials to make simple things
- Use simple hand tools, materials and components

National Curriculum coverage in design and technology

Design cycle phases

- **Identifying needs and opportunities** Pupils will be able to describe to others and imagine solutions to problems and ask questions to help identify needs

- **Generating designs** Children will be able to express their ideas about meeting needs

- **Planning and making** Use a variety of materials and equipment to make simple things and show that they can use simple hand tools, materials and components

- **Evaluating** Describe to others what they have done and what they like and dislike about familiar artefacts and systems

103

The programme of study

- **Developing and using artefacts, systems and environments** Children will know that a system is made of related parts and they will be able to identify which parts of protective packaging do which job

- **Working with materials** Children will have a complete range of experiences including exploring and using a variety of materials, joining materials and components and using equipment safely

- **Developing and communicating ideas** Children will use imagination and their own experiences to generate and explore ideas

- **Satisfying needs and addressing opportunities** Children will evaluate their finished work against the original intentions

Cross-curricular coverage

- **English** Starting point: *Postman Pat* story , writing skills enhanced through self-evaluation, discussion in groups over options

- **Information technology** (AT5) *Postman Pat* program

- **Mathematics** Measuring, estimating, area, two- and three-dimensional shapes

- **Science** Weight

Introduction

Taking six to eight weeks to complete, this topic has been based upon storytelling sessions about *Postman Pat*. Many design and technology activities can be drawn from the postal service. They can include packaging, protective clothing and many forms of communications. In order to make the most of such potential it is very important to be prepared to guide your pupils with an appropriate questioning approach.

Getting started

As in all work it is necessary to build upon previous experience and to take account of the levels within the class. It would be useful to introduce the practical activities that are at the centre of this topic by reading stories such as *Postman Pat*. During the storytelling it is possible to ask pertinent questions like:

- How heavy is Postman Pat's sack?

- Do things get broken in the post?
- How can you protect fragile items?
- How long does it take to deliver a parcel?
- How much does it cost to send a letter or a parcel?
- Why do some things cost more to send than others?

Relevant activities might include:

- Visiting the local Post Office
- Designing and making an envelope
- Studying different packing materials
- Weighing parcels
- Wrapping parcels of different shapes
- Posting carefully packed fragile items
- Examining the received fragile items
- Evaluating the success and failure of their work.

Engaging in these activites will ensure that there is a well prepared background upon which your young pupils can build. This topic is ideally situated in the second part of the autumn term, leading up to Christmas. Links with your local Post Office will make the topic much more real and will inspire your pupils and provide plenty of opportunities for evaluation.

Resources and classroom organisation

Pupils will work in groups, pairs and occasionally individually, with rotation between practical work areas and quiet areas. Your pupils can bring in a selection of fragile items and also junk materials including packaging materials from home. You will need to provide scissors, Sellotape, glue, wrapping paper, polystyrene pieces, foam, cotton wool (dampened to keep plant alive), newspaper, wood sticks, bubble material, card, boxes, coloured paper rulers, paint and pencils, books and other information about the work of the Royal Mail.

Activities

Three main activities can be used:

- Design and make an envelope
- Wrap differently shaped parcels
- Pack up a delicate object, such as a bottle of perfume, light bulb, pot plant.

In the first activity children can explore the various designs of envelopes, opening out and understanding the construction of nets and the way different materials behave and can be used. The children will use various sheets of coloured paper (of the same size), Sellotape as a sealant and scissors; this exercise invariably involves deep thought and complex folding.

In the packing of different shaped parcels, the understanding of shape will progress from two- and three-dimensional solids. Again you will be able to open out wrappings and compare with the three-dimensional solids.

If you use a number of different types of fragile objects then each group will have some individual problems to overcome. Common considerations will be the need to reduce the weight of all packages to keep the cost of posting down to a minimum. Groups will discuss how to approach the task of labelling each parcel: should it say, for example, *Do not Bang* or *Fragile*? Naturally all labels would have to clearly prepared. Children need to think about such questions as how big the letters should be and what colour they should be printed in.

Your children will have to consider how tight a fit is best, how to pack the empty space and how to move from the design to the making stage most easily. In this we have found that Checkpaper and Checkcard are excellent from practical and economic points of view.

Once the parcels have been completed, use your connections with the Post Office to have the parcels delivered to your school. On arrival your pupils will have ample opportunity for a final evaluation session involving all groups, individuals and yourself.

Recording

You can collect up all the envelopes, make comments, including the pupils' own remarks, date and place them in your pupils' own folios. Photograph important elements of the three-dimensional work, annotate these and place them in the folio. Use your own system of recording pupils' progress; evaluate the topic for future reference.

You will find that there will be considerable discussion about the materials to be used, the best approach to tackling the tasks, how to protect the objects – especially the plants. Besides the obvious strength of the topic from the design and technology perspective, it offers great opportunities for English and mathematics.

Design and Technology Web – The post KS 2

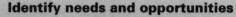

Identify needs and opportunities

- From evaluation identify weak and strong points of clothing
- Take account of delivery systems and human factors

Evaluate

- Existing protective clothing
- Letter sorting systems
- New products as 2nd evaluation stage

Design and Technology Cycle

Generate designs

- Working from sketches, use patterns and fabrics for designs
- Experiment with various designs

Plan and make

- Using waterproof materials make jacket or delivery bag
- Make simple mechanisms to sort sizes of letters

National Curriculum coverage in design and technology

Design cycle phases

- **Identifying needs and opportunities** Pupils start with familiar situations and develop and clarify their ideas through discussion with those involved. Pupils will also devise ways of gathering data, recognise the points of view of others and use market information

- **Generating designs** Discuss the reasoning behind design proposals, make designs, use models and sketches, estimate resource requirements and record the progress of their ideas showing how they have clarified them

- **Planning and making** Look at waterproofing and sorting mechanisms

- **Evaluating** This work starts with an evaluation of existing protective clothing and letter sorting systems. The evaluative processes are completed when the children's own designs are put to the test at the end of the design cycle

The programme of study

- **Developing and using artefacts, systems and environments** Pupils will organise and plan their work, allocate time and resources effectively, use a variety of information sources. They will be taught to use equipment safely, select the right materials, join and assemble materials avoiding wastage and finish work carefully

- **Developing and communicating ideas** Children will be taught to take account of other people's reactions to aesthetic characteristics, produce plans and drawings using a range of graphics materials

- **Satisfying needs and opportunities** Children will develop understanding of the need for complete market awareness, they will discuss with 'clients,' take account of costs, try to ensure that their designs satisfy the perceived needs

Cross-curricular coverage

- **English** Discussion in class and with Post Office staff. The writing of questionnaires, understanding the need for carefully constructed sentences. Writing evaluations, preparing designs, annotation

- **Information technology** Use word processor for producing questionnaires, use simple analysis package to present results in pie-charts and bar-graphs

- **Mathematics** Measuring, symmetry, pattern-making, calculations, graph work

- **Science** Use of existing knowledge about how to make things move and make them waterproof if necessary

- **Art and design** Graphic design and textile work

Introduction

This is a natural extension to the previous infant level topic. An effective stimulus to the series of activities given below can be the visit to your school of the local postman or woman, or a visit to the sorting office. Unlike most of the other topics in this bank, here we start from the evaluation phase of the design cycle. Children are asked to consider the suitability of a postman's uniform and methods of handling and sorting letters. After a discussion with the visiting postman or woman a list of strong and weak points is

produced. It is particularly helpful to build a long-term relationship with the postman so that advice and guidance can be gathered throughout the topic. Pupils then work up designs and finally make uniforms and simple letter sorting systems. These are then evaluated.

Getting started

As mentioned above, this topic starts with the evaluating phase of the design cycle and in the cycle shown there are two specific evaluation stages. This does not mean, of course, that evaluation is finite and tied to specific points of the design cycle; it is a continuous process.

A visit to your local sorting office may bring many things to mind; in the example that we offer here two specific issues are dealt with:

- How to make improvements to the design of protective clothing and post bags
- How to deal with the sorting of letters in a small local Post Office.

Resources and classroom organisation

Pupils will work in groups or pairs. Most practical activities will need dry working conditions. Textiles and waterproofing will need a special preparation for working with water. The resources you will need to provide include needles, a range of textiles, wax and other safe waterproofing materials, balsa wood, glues, paper and fixing components. Construction kits such as Meccano, Lego and Fischertechnik will also be needed.

Activities

- Examining existing garments and systems
- Gathering a range of information from books/magazines
- Designing and using a questionnaire with local Post Office staff
- Analysing and using the results from the questionnaire in design proposals
- Designing and making
  – protective clothing or post bag
  – a simple machine for sorting envelopes according to size.

In the first activity children can talk with Post Office staff about their clothes, asking questions about their suitability and whether or not they like the designs. Gathering information is very important and you will need to ensure that the right range of books and magazines is available.

In the third activity, children will have to crystallise their thoughts about the design tasks and construct a questionnaire which they will then be able to use to gather further, more detailed information from a number of Post Office workers.

Before becoming involved in designing and making, your pupils will have to analyse and use the results from the questionnaire.

In designing and making many practical activities will be involved. Here, by referring to the programme of study, we think you will get a clear idea of the scope and depth of the activities.

Developing and using artefacts, systems and environments Your pupils will be required to organise and plan their work carefully, introducing new ideas, so that their work improves. They will have to plan how their practical activities may be organised and will need to use a variety of information sources in developing their work. Finally they will identify the parts of a system and their functions, and use this knowledge to inform their designing and making activities.

Working with materials Children will use equipment safely, select materials for their task, join materials in semi-permanent forms and eventually assemble materials using a variety of means. By controlling the amount of materials that are made available they will be encouraged to avoid wastage and finish work carefully.

Developing and communicating ideas In the activities described the pupils will be required to cover some ground from key stage 1. They will represent and develop ideas by drawings and models, and through talking, writing and working with materials. Because of the research requirements within the National Curriculum they will also need to find out, sort, store and present information for use in their designing and making activities. As they will be working with knowledge of the preferences of local Post Office staff they should take account of their reactions to aesthetic characteristics. Because of the various stages in the processes they will need to plan and structure their communication of ideas and proposals. Also they will use drawings and plans to investigate and develop ideas for three-dimensional objects. As part of these activities they will use a range of graphic techniques and processes, and use modelling to explore design and technological ideas. By working in pairs or groups the teams can break design tasks into sub-tasks and focus on each in turn as a way of developing ideas while they use materials and equipment to produce results which are aesthetically pleasing.

Satisfying needs and addressing opportunities Having conducted market research, your children will know that the needs and preferences of consumers influence the design and production of goods and services. As they are not able to use unlimited resources, the children will come to recognise the importance of consumer choice and hence the importance of product quality and cost. Further they will be aware that the appearance of artefacts and environments is important to consumers and users. Because the artefacts are being designed as clothes or machines to be operated by Post Office staff,

human shape, scale, proportion and movement will affect the forms of designs. If questions are included in the questionnaire that are to do with unit costs of jackets, it is likely that your pupils will understand that goods may be designed to be produced singly or in quantity, and that this affects what each item costs. They will need to plan, evaluate and adjust their work as they progress.

Once the newly designed garments and letter sorters are complete, you may wish to invite your local postman or woman to give their opinions as part of the final evaluation stage.

Recording

The first element of the activities is the evaluation of existing artefacts and systems; this stage needs to be recorded. Your pupils' written accounts, however brief, can be accompanied by their sketches and kept in their folios. Your pupils' work in identifying needs can be observed in their discussions and recorded by you on prepared stationery. It is particularly likely that the processes involved in the designing, making and planning activities will be best recorded by photography. The photographs, when dated and annotated, should be filed with the children's other work.

Design and Technology Web – Clothes KS 1

Identify needs and opportunities

Set problems by teacher
- Identify different needs for clothes
- Take existing shoes and design a new pair

Evaluate

- A pair of shoes from cardboard
- A hat
- A woven pattern
- Dyes
- Joseph's coat

Design and Technology Cycle

Generate designs

- For a pair of shoes from cardboard
- For a hat
- For a woven pattern
- For Joseph's coat

Plan and make

- A pair of shoes from cardboard
- A hat
- A woven pattern
- Dyes from tissue paper
- Joseph's coat of many colours

National Curriculum coverage in design and technology

Design cycle phases

- **Identifying needs and opportunities** Children will start to understand that clothes need to fit their purposes for durability, colour, waterproofing, fireproofing, and so on

- **Generating designs** The problems will require both designing and making. These will include the use of computer programs, such as *Mosaic*, and producing designs for shoes and hats

- **Planning and making** Making clothes using a variety of materials

- **Evaluating** Children will be required to produce workable designs, and as such they can be evaluated easily

The programme of study

- **Developing and using artefacts, systems and environments** Developing a system of dyeing

- **Working with materials** Dyes, vinegar, papers, cards, glues, graphic materials, wax, oil, fabrics, textiles

- **Developing and communicating ideas** Writing about clothes and techniques for making clothes

- **Satisfying needs and addressing opportunities** Solving the set problems

Cross-curricular coverage

- **English** Imaginative writing of plays and stories, descriptive writing about fabric types and clothes for different purposes. Stimulus: *Mrs Mopple's Washing Line* and *Joseph's Story*

- **Art** Observational drawings of clothes and fabrics under microscopes, dyeing, painting, designing. Observational full-scale drawings of children to compare actual sizes. Weaving using card strips and a range of fabrics. Colour

- **Information technology** Using computer to write about clothes and fabric, about uniforms and protective clothing, using pattern programs such as *Mosaic* to emulate woven structures

- **Mathematics** Comparison of sizes (shoe and hat sizes), shape (two- and three-dimensional)

- **Science** Waterproofing, using microscopes and magnifying glasses, making solutions and fixing dyes with vinegar. Structures – flexible and rigid materials. Colour. Staining fabric to make coat

Introduction

We have based this topic upon one that started with the wedding of a sister of one of the children in the class concerned. The class of six-year-olds became fascinated by the idea of making special clothes for all kinds of special occasions, including making hats and masks for fancy dress parties. There are, of course, many ways of introducing topics on clothing, through stories, celebrations or the services such as the post, police, ambulance or fire service.

Work on clothing, if set at the right level, can be very enjoyable and many of the most important aspects of design and technology can be covered by setting problems such as:

- Design and make a pair of shoes that can be worn and used for walking over a measured distance – say 20 metres
- Design and make a hat to wear to a fancy dress party
- Design a woven pattern
- Make and use dyes made from tissue papers, vinegar and water
- Design and make Joseph's coat of many colours.

During such tasks children can evaluate their successes and failures, modifying their work as they go along. Introducing clothing in this way will allow children to progress naturally and develop creative and critical faculties.

Getting started

Discussions about weddings or other special events can be directed towards special clothes and religious stories, while work on fabrics, dyes, shoes, hats and religious dramas can be developed. Questions about how clothes and other products are coloured can be led towards work on making dyes from tissue paper. Of course you may need to supplement these with a range of cold water dyes such as Dylon. Below we refer to making Joseph's coat of many colours; you may feel happy to take this on literally; however if constraints are too great, then children can make clay models and make up small simple costumes for the dolls.

This topic and similar ones have been used with groups of five- to six-year-olds over periods of approximately six weeks.

Resources and classroom organisation

You will need drawing paper, a selection of pencils, felt tip pens, fabrics and samples, buttons, sequins, sewing equipment, glues and other graphic materials. Magnifying glasses and microscopes will be useful. Protective aprons and lots of newspaper are essential. You should collect visual stimulus material and relevant books, fashion magazines and catalogues. Also collect examples of clothing and shoes with different fastenings (buttons, zips, hooks and eyes, buckles, laces, poppers, Velcro, and so on).

Activities

- Making hats
- Making dyes using water, tissue paper and vinegar

A variety of activities can support this topic

- Using the dyes to do tie-and-dye work with different fabrics
- Making up a play about Joseph and his coat of many colours, designing and painting the backdrop for the play
- Choosing the right size clothes for each child in the play
- Comparing different thread thicknesses, looking at different fabrics using magnifying glass
- Writing about clothes worn by different professions such as firemen, ambulance drivers and clergy
- Weaving with strips of card of equal length
- Using computer programs such as *Mosaic* to design weave patterns.

Recording

Collect plans, drawings, sketches and written work, make selections and file the samples in children's folios.

Clothes key stage 2

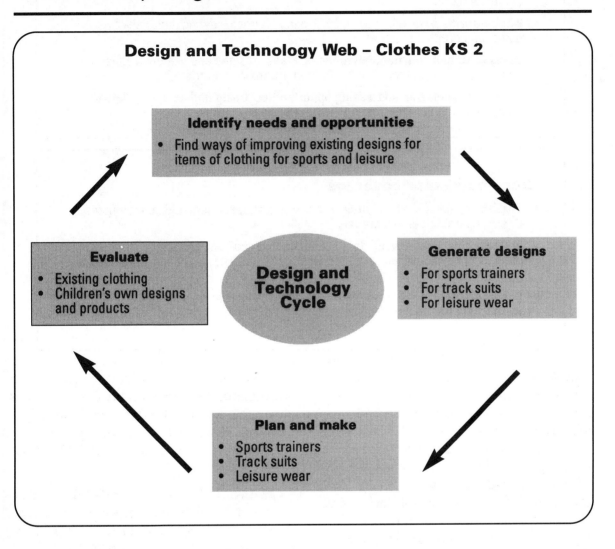

Design and Technology Web – Clothes KS 2

Identify needs and opportunities
- Find ways of improving existing designs for items of clothing for sports and leisure

Design and Technology Cycle

Generate designs
- For sports trainers
- For track suits
- For leisure wear

Evaluate
- Existing clothing
- Children's own designs and products

Plan and make
- Sports trainers
- Track suits
- Leisure wear

National Curriculum coverage in design and technology

Design cycle phases

- **Identifying needs and opportunities** Use questionnaires to find ways of improving existing designs, taking account of costs and marketing requirements

- **Generating designs** Shoes, track suits and leisure wear

- **Planning and making** Models and prototypes for shoes, track suits and leisure wear

- **Evaluating** Existing products and children's own designs

Cross-curricular coverage

- **English** Writing questionnaires, interviewing shopkeepers and school-mates. Designing promotional materials

- **Mathematics** Graph work, data collection and analysis, pattern and template work, nets, solid and two-dimensional shapes and forms. Scaling from plans to finished work, measuring and calculation

- **Science** Colour, dyes (from plants), structure, weather, heat (keeping warm/cool), our bodies (movement)

Introduction

As children reach top junior levels they will already have had experience of designing and making clothes. Those clothes may have been made for toys, for the pupils themselves or as part of history topics on Greeks, Romans, the Victorians and so on. As children build and extend their skills they will be able to tackle more demanding tasks. The topic offered below contains examples of design and technology tasks suitable for top juniors and extends their economic awareness.

Getting started

This topic is intended to give children the chance of designing and making trainers or sportswear such as tracksuits or sweatshirts that they think could be made up into commercially viable products. It is most likely that garments will be produced as prototypes. However if you manage to get substantial help from local tradespeople you may find that it is feasible to make up a few finished items. Such products could be sold to support school funds or charitable activities.

Children will need to undertake market research before becoming involved in designing and making activities. Contact local fashion and sports shops with the aim of visiting shops and having staff visit your school. Children will need to find out about which features, such as price, design, colour, quality, durability, fashion and brand names, help sell particular garments.

Resources and classroom organisation

You will need drawing paper, Checkcard, card, junk materials (corrugated cardboard),

114

selection of pencils, felt-tip pens, fabrics and samples, buttons and fastenings of all kinds (including Velcro), sewing equipment, glues (possibly a glue gun), a collection of patterns, visual material (fashion magazines and catalogues) and examples of clothing and shoes.

We recommend that children complete this work in pairs.

Activities

Meeting with tradespeople and salespeople will involve informal discussions and the use of interview schedules or questionnaires. When designing questionnaires (however simple), collecting data and analysing it you should ask your children to consider:

- Colour
- Weather and seasonal considerations
- Will the clothes be suitable for boys and girls alike?
- Cost of making

- Do people like existing designs?
- Practicability.

When children have decided which garment they would like to produce they will be involved in sketching and designing the chosen garment. They will also make patterns, select fabrics, dyes and fasteners. You should make sure your pupils have the opportunity of observing and analysing different types and styles of clothing.

Recording

Children should be encouraged to make a few notes about visits to sports/fashion shops and write these up as a basis for preparing questionnaires. The results from analysing responses to questions and evidence of the different stages should be recorded. Photographs of finished products (and flat layout plans) should be dated, annotated and filed in children's folios.

The design cycle in action

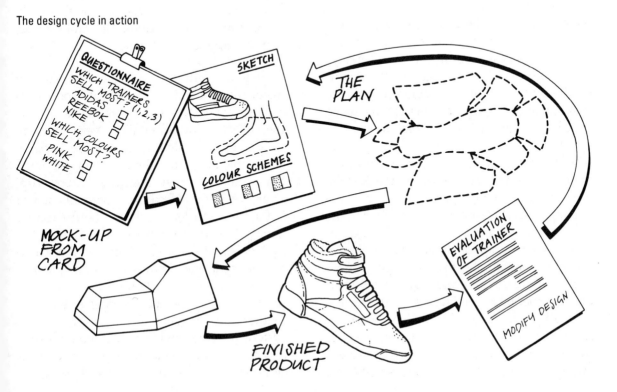

5

A GUIDE TO COMPONENTS, MATERIALS AND TOOLS

Components, materials and tools are central to children's development. It is through their use that the important skills and concepts of design and technology are developed. They must, however, be phased in gradually. Some materials and a number of tools will not be appropriate for very young children, but, in a good school, a wide range will be in use by the later stages of primary schooling.

Children need to be guided towards an understanding of the properties of materials through exploration, trial and adjustment, building, shaping and so on. The range of materials available in infant classrooms needs to be carefully considered in order to ensure that children gain experience of using as wide a variety as possible. It is often assumed that by the time they come to school children will have made mud-pies, built sandcastles, or helped in the kitchen mixing and rolling pastry, and perhaps making gingerbread figures. However many will have missed out on these vital experiences. One reception class teacher in a Rochdale school notes that, 'A large number of the children in my class will not have had these experiences which we think are commonplace. They will not have been on holiday, or worked with a grown-up making cakes, digging the garden or helping to clean out the shed. I see it as my responsibility that this is remedied by the things we do at school.'

Materials for very young children should be easy to work and adaptable in meeting the needs of each child's imagination. For example, cardboard tubes can be used for towers, bodies, legs, telescopes, wheels and rollers. Cardboard boxes can be buildings, boats, animal bodies, and so on. Ready-made resources such as wheels can, at this early stage, impose ideas upon the child rather than encourage inventiveness.

Modelling with waste materials plays a major role in children's practical experiences during this early stage. In many classrooms the collection of materials is very random; nearly all discarded materials are seen as acceptable and often deposited in one large bin. Children then adopt a 'lucky dip' approach to the selection of materials, which is far from satisfactory. It can be frustrating having to sort through too wide a range of materials and container shapes in the search for the right one. Some schools have identified the most needed junk materials and provide lists for parents in order to ensure a regular supply. A well-organised storage system provides children with comparisons and choices invaluable in the growth of decision-making, categorising and sorting skills.

In the following parts of this chapter we have drawn together information about the range of components, materials and tools that you will need for design and technology activities. Each area is accompanied by a checklist which is cross-referred to key stages 1 and 2.

A dictionary of components

Balloons

These are ideal as sources of propulsion power for light vehicles. They are available in a variety of shapes, sizes and colours.

Clothes pegs

Clothes pegs can be used for holding materials together temporarily. They can be used as clamps, axle guides or incorporated as parts of models or mechanisms. They can also be used to hang printed or painted sheets for drying.

Corks

Corks are very useful in floating and sinking topics because of their buoyancy. In a more limited way corks may be modelled. Reconstituted cork discs are also useful.

Cotton reels

Standard and small cotton reels are now usually made from plastic, although wooden ones are still available. They are very useful as wide pulley wheels or winding drums for cranes. They can also be used as wheels or as parts of mechnisms.

Elastic bands

These can be used as pulley belts and as excellent devices for storing energy when the elastic is stretched or twisted. The potential energy is released as the band is allowed to assume its original length.

Electrical components

Batteries These come in a variety of physical sizes and voltage ratings, and you can

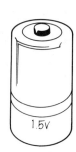

Checklist of components

Balloons	*Fasteners, clips and pins*
Clothes pegs	Gears
Corks	Lolly sticks
Cotton reels	*Marbles*
Elastic bands	Matchsticks
Electrical components:	*Pipe cleaners*
Batteries	Propellors
Battery holders and clips	Pulleys
Bulbs	Springs
Bulb holders	*Straws*
Buzzers	Syringes
Connectors	*Wheels*
Motors	
Sensors and switches	*Items in italics are particularly suitable for KS1*

choose rechargeable types. It is important to match the voltage outputs from batteries to the energy requirements of motors and other devices. If you use a 12-volt battery to run a 6-volt motor then you are likely to burn out the motor. Too low a voltage battery will not be able to make a highly-rated device work properly or at all. Rechargeable batteries require a charger unit and initially do cost more. However over a period of time considerable savings can be made.

Battery holders and clips These can be used to combine batteries and result in power supplies that correspond to the individual voltgages added together. Some batteries require holders to be connected using battery snaps of the type that connects square batteries with twin top terminals.

Bulbs Small bulbs that are miniature Edison screw (MES) have screw threaded shafts, not bayonet, and are available in a number of voltages. Here it is important to match

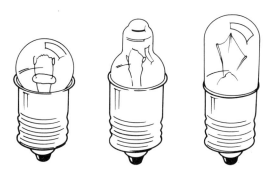

battery and bulb voltages. They are ideal for lighting models or for fair testing devices.

Bulb holders These can be obtained as 'batten' or clip-on types. Batten holders can be screwed to a firm surface and have screw terminals to receive connecting wires. The clip-on type are useful as they are less obtrusive and can be quickly fixed and moved from thin section material like lolly sticks. These have solder terminals, although if you do not wish to solder the connecting wires you can simply bare sufficient of the connecting wires, thread these through the terminal tags and tape them in place.

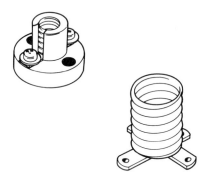

Buzzers These can be used wherever a sound source is needed as an alarm or signal. They are usually supplied with short lengths of lead wires attached and produce a variety of sounds.

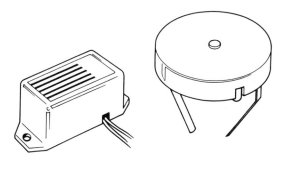

Connectors 'Crocodile clips' are the most common type of electrical connector. As their name suggests they are spring loaded metal jaws. To one extension of the jaw is a terminal (screw or solder) to which wires can be connected. The metal jaws ensure electrical contact. Often the leads and clip are insulated with plastic. Other types of connectors such as spade, wanda and ring connectors require the right kind of sockets or plugs to complete circuits. Small extension connectors are useful for when you wish to keep a 'set-up' while making different use of batteries.

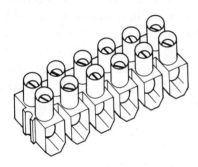

Motors A small electric motor can bring life to models that require some form of motion. Most electric motors have 2 mm diameter drive shafts that rotate at speeds of more than 1000 revolutions per minute. This is far too high for most applications. It is necessary to control and reduce the speed by a form of 'gearing down' (see *Gears*).

Gearbox motors allow changes to be made to the ratios within an integrated gearbox and

vary the speed of the drive shaft between 2000 and 2 rpm. For plotters and programmable machines where fine control is essential you will need to use stepper motors. Gearbox and stepper motors are much more expensive than simple miniature electric motors.

Sensors There are two common types of sensors generally available:

- LDR (or photoresistors) – light dependent resistors
- TDR (or thermistors) – temperature dependent resistors.

These alter their internal electrical resistance within given ranges of light and temperature intensities. This means that they can set off other devices, such as alarms or mechanisms, because of changes in light or temperature. Other forms of sensors are pressure pads. Thermistors are the least expensive of sensors.

Switches These provide basic control in electrical circuits. There are eight main types: toggle, tilt, rocker, push, relays, micro-switches, slide and reed switches. They are operated either physically or by their switching action within the circuit. The simplest type is the 'single pole single throw' (spst): these are make-or-break, fixed on/off switches. Other physical switches such as push button are operated by continuous pressure; once released the internal spring returns them to their original position. Push switches and certain types of reed switches are the cheapest, while relays, toggle and tilt switches tend to be more expensive.

Single pole switches can also be 'double throw' (spdt). These have two 'on' positions and sometimes a third 'off' position. In this way a single switch can be used to activate two different circuits or parts of a circuit. Double throw switches are sometimes referred to as 'changeovers'. You will find that these switches are most useful in circuits that run motors. They can be used to reverse the polarity of supply to the motor and so change its direction of rotation. Other specialised switches include reed switches, in which two thin strips of metal can be made either to make or break contact with each other, usually by the proximity or absence of a magnet.

Tilt switches consist of a small glass bulb in which a small drop of mercury can move freely and make contact between terminals when the switch is upright. In any other position, no contact is made and the switch is off.

Other switches that are activated by electric currents are called relays. These can be used in remote control devices and are activated by sensors, thereafter switching on a circuit containing a motor or other device.

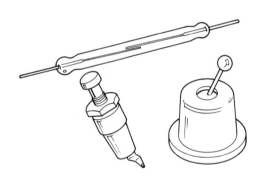

Fasteners, clips and pins

A wide range of fasteners, clips and pins is available to fix and join materials permanently or temporarily. The most useful will be paper clips, drawing pins, dressmaking pins, brass paper fasteners and bulldog clips.

Gears

Gears are used to transfer motion from one place to another and to change the direction,

speed and type of motion. Many of these operations can happen simultaneously.

Cog wheels (wheels with teeth around their circumferences) are used widely in gear systems. Gear wheels vary in size to accommodate different numbers of teeth. It is easy to understand that two gear wheels of equal size with the same number of teeth will transfer motion with no change in speed while the direction of motion is reversed. If the number of teeth (and thus the diameter) on one of the gear wheels is reduced then the smaller wheel will turn faster. The difference in speed is directly related to the ratio of teeth on one wheel to another. For example, twice as many teeth will reduce speed by half, a quarter as many teeth will result in four times the speed.

Bevel and worm gears can be used to change the direction or plane of the motion. Bevel gears are gear wheels with the teeth set at angles, usually 45 degrees. Therefore if you use two bevels together, you can change direction of motion through 90 degrees.

Worm gears are, effectively, a screw thread that can be meshed with a gear wheel to change the direction of motion through 90 degrees. Worm gears are normally driven imparting the motion to the gear wheels rather than vice-versa.

Gear racks (as used in many car steering and windscreen wiper mechanisms) can be used to transfer the rotary motion from an electric motor spindle into a linear motion.

Axles are slotted into the holes at the centre of gear wheels; these holes are normally either 2 or 4 mm. 2 mm holes allow the gears to be push-fitted onto the spindles of most electric motors. 4 mm will allow fitting onto wooden dowels. Meccano and Fischertechnik have excellent and sophisticated systems. The range of wheels that you will need will include those listed overleaf.

- ³/₃₂ inch gear wheels with brass hub and grub screw, with 10–60 teeth
- Gear wheels, 2 and 4 mm central holes, plastic, 10–60 teeth
- Gear wheels, 4 mm hole with grub screw, nylon, 10–60 teeth
- Gear wheels, 4 mm hole, large diameter, PVC, 10–58 teeth
- Worm gears, ³/₃₂ inch with brass hubs and grub screws
- Worm gears, 2 and 4mm central holes
- Bevel gears, 45 degrees, ³/₃₂ inch brass hub with grub screw
- Bevel gears, 45 degrees 2 and 4mm holes
- Gear racks, 100 mm

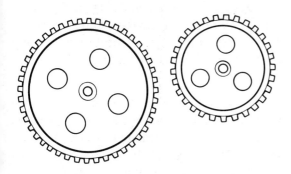

Lolly sticks

These are available in three sizes (including large tongue depressors) and are a useful modelling material. They have particular applications as linkages, wheel spokes, teeth for gear wheels and for mounting light bulb holders.

Marbles

These lend themselves very well to investigations of rolling motion and, of course, can be used as bearings between surfaces. Most common marbles are available in 14 mm and 19 mm diameter sizes.

Matchsticks

Headless matches are a useful modelling material.

Pipe cleaners

These are available in assorted colours. They can be used as ties to fix materials, as flexible linkages, simple hinges and as parts of many types of models.

Propellers

Usually made from plastic with two or three blades, propellers are used as a means of propulsion for light models. They can be driven by electric motors or elastic bands.

Pulleys

Pulleys are grooved wheels that offer a method of transferring rotary motion with an ability to change the speed of rotation. The relative diameter of pulley wheels determines the speed at which they turn. Pulley wheels of equal diameter transfer motion with no change in speed. You will notice that pulley wheels rotate in the same direction.

If you reduce the diameter of one pulley wheel you will increase its rotary speed, and vice-versa. The difference in diameters relates directly to the speed of pulleys used in the same system.

Pulley wheels can be converted to 'friction drivers' by adding a rubber ring into the groove of the pulley wheel. The rubber ring

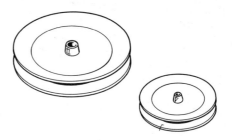

is called an 'O' ring. Such friction drivers can be applied directly to the surface of a wheel or drum that you wish to rotate. Wheels and drums rotate in the opposite direction to the friction driver.

Pulleys are available with 2 and 4mm holes, made from plastic and brass.

Springs

Springs can be usefully used to store and release energy in all kinds of mechanisms. Compression springs have a naturally open form while extension springs are naturally closed. Steel springs are available in 4 and 6 mm diameters and can be purchased in assorted packs of compression and extension springs.

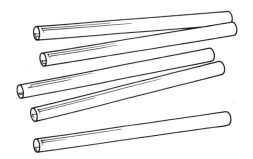

Straws

These are an excellent basic modelling material. They can also be used as spindles and axles. The 4mm diameter sizes fit the central holes of standard pulley and gear wheels. There are several types available; 'bendy straws' have a concertina section which allows straws to be bent without buckling, plastic straws are stronger, while non-waxed paper ones are easier to paint or colour with felt pens. Artstraws (non-waxed paper) are available in 4, 6 and 10mm diameters.

Syringes

Syringes are plastic and always supplied without needles. These offer a simple introduction to elementary pneumatics and hydraulics when used in conjunction with plastic tubing.

Using different sized syringes will change the pressure output or the degree of movement. Generally a larger output syringe will give less movement but a larger force, and vice-versa.

The increase in force is equal to the increase in cross-sectional area of the syringe, that is, twice the area is equivalent to twice the force. If you use syringes of the same length with known volume it is easy to calculate the ratio of cross-sectional areas. Syringes are available in 50, 20, 10, 5, 2 and 1 millilitre sizes.

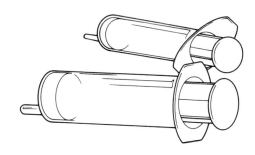

Wheels

Wheels are available in many sizes and from many materials. They also have a wide range of central hole sizes. Common materials are card, wood and plastic. When you choose materials for axles make sure you relate the diameter and hole sizes and the need for a tight or loose fit.

Materials

The National Curriculum document for design and technology requires that:

> " At each key stage pupils should be given the opportunities to work with a range of materials, including textiles, graphic media such as paint, paper, photographs, construction materials such as clay, wood, plastic, metal and food."
>
> Technology in the National Curriculum (DES, HMSO. 1990)

It is the conscious and appropriate inter-relating of materials, concepts and contexts that can allow most effectively for progression and development. We have found that before planning progression the first step needs to be the categorisation of materials. For example, construction materials can be categorised as follows:

- Sheet materials – paper, card, foil, metal
- Malleable materials – dough, plasticine, clay
- Resistant materials – wood, acrylic, metal
- Compound materials – pastry, plaster, concrete.

It is helpful to apply this approach to other materials:

- Textiles
- Graphic materials
- Components (electrical bulbs, batteries, switches)
- Mechanical fasteners
- Springs
- Wheels and axles
- Food.

Progression in these materials is supported by necessary tools, resources and equipment appropriate to each level of development.

The listing of materials below is not exhaustive. When you add to the list and offer materials for use in class, try to ensure that the characteristics of the materials match the requirements of the activity to be undertaken. The properties of a material determine its basic use and the ways in which it can be shaped, formed, fixed and joined.

Checklist of materials

Card (Checkcard and Checkpaper)
Clay (and other malleable materials)
Metal
Plastics
Textiles
Wood

Items in italics are particularly suitable for KS1

A dictionary of materials

Card

Nearly all consumer products are formed, at least in part, from sheet materials. A material such as card provides an excellent means of entering the consumer world. It can be folded, bent, cut, formed, made into boxes, and can be used to represent room layouts and for architecture and vehicle design. Beyond these, it may be used to construct cylinders and all kinds of mathematical shapes; it represents an excellent means of coming to terms with design in its broadest sense.

Card is a very versatile sheet modelling material. Available in a variety of thicknesses; thick card is stiff, rigid and strong, while thinner material is flexible. Most card, apart from the thicker types, can be cut with scissors. Utility snips and craft knives make the best cutting tools for thicker materials. Card is an excellent material for a number of attainment targets; its flexibility enables it to be folded and rolled and, when laminated, it is transformed into a material of greater strength. Card can be fixed in a number of ways: PVA is particularly good when applied in thin skims (applied by squeegee action of the edge of another piece of card), or when applied to specific points; a little patience is needed in making a precise and firm join; double-sided Sellotape, staples, pins and ordinary Sellotape can also be used in certain situations.

You can find card in many forms. Cardboard boxes and tubes are commonly found in the collections of junk materials in schools. These offer pre-formed shapes, which can be difficult for young children to make, but which are fundamental to many designing and making activities. Given a wide selection of junk or 'found' materials that are well organised, children can make discriminating choices about size and shape and will also be able to adapt, cut and extend existing boxes and tubes to suit their purpose. Some cardboard containers can have additional characteristics such as being waxed; such containers have a degree of water-proofing.

A particularly useful material that has recently been developed is available under the brand names of 'Checkcard' and 'Checkpaper'. The basic material, accurately printed 1 cm squares on SRA2 high quality card and cartridge paper, in a variety of colours, is accompanied by excellent curriculum materials that follow a cross-curricular approach while focussing on design and technology. Work cards are also available.

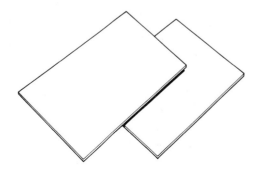

Clay (and other malleable materials)

Clay and plasticine offer your pupils opportunities for working in different malleable materials. The qualities of clay are very attractive to children. Given the right preparation it need not be too messy, although it can cause problems with the dust it produces. The fact that clay hardens as it dries and is fired in a kiln, while plasticine becomes more easily worked when warm, should be ex-ploited in class.

Metal

This is available in the form of wire that is flexible, comparatively strong and is an electrical conductor. Use wire cutters or pliers for cutting wire. Don't use scissors as they will be damaged. Wire can be used in many ways in designing and making activities. It can be easily formed, wound into springs or bent into hooks or rings.

Metal rods are stronger than wooden dowels and they can be used as axles or pivots. Rods can also be bent to form cranks. It is best to use vices to hold rods firmly while cutting with hacksaws.

Sheet metal is usually found as aluminium foil, which can be torn, rolled, folded and made into many shapes. Aluminium and steel sheets can be used. The latter are strong and if you wish to cut them you will need a hacksaw. It is essential that the metal sheet is held firmly in a vice for cutting. Sheet aluminium can be bent accurately if it is held firmly in a vice with the line of bend juxtaposed with blocks of wood as a sandwich on both sides of the sheet. With another block of wood bend the sheet to the required angle with the help of a wooden mallet if necessary.

Meccano offers an excellent way of using metal for many younger pupils. Your pupils can, alternatively, overlap pieces of cut sheet metal that can be joined with nuts and bolts through pre-drilled holes.

Safety is a prime concern when using metal. Cut metal will often have jagged or burred edges. If you ensure that sharp edges and corners are blunted by using metal files then you will reduce danger to a minimum.

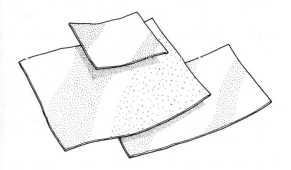

Plastics

There are many different types of plastics, each with its own characteristics. PVC is generally not environmentally friendly and we would caution against its use. Plastic in fluted form, such as Correx and Corriflute, like a laminated corrugated cardboard, is an attractive material as it has enhanced strength and is relatively light. However, it is important not to latch on to materials that seem to be easy to use. We have seen more inappropriate uses of Corriflute than of any other material. It is also worth examining carefully the cost per square metre that is charged by the various suppliers.

Other types of plastics that are available are:

Bextrene High impact polystyrene sheets. This is an extruded sheet which has either a smooth matt or highly polished surface. It is relatively easy to cut and is good for making shadow puppets.

Britannia A light foam board, a strong coated board-faced foam sandwich-type board. Available in 3, 5 and 10mm thicknesses.

Corribond Adhesive tape for bonding sheets together, particularly useful for Correx and Corriflute.

Doeflex An extremely tough polypropylene, excellent for making containers. It die-cuts well and produces good creases with superb flex strength.

Foam pads Foam coated on both surfaces with an aggressive, pressure sensitive, high-tack acrylic adhesive.

Magnetic rubber A gloss white faced magnetic synthetic rubber, easily cut for many applications.

Special care needs to be taken when using plastics. PVC, polythene and Correx are thermosetting plastics which will melt uncontrollably and, in some cases, give off toxic fumes when heated.

Like card, plastics can be found in preformed shapes of containers and bottles in collected junk materials.

Plastic fibres such as nylon thread or fishing line are far stronger than cotton threads of similar diameter, although they can be rather more difficult to tie because the knots tend to slip.

Textiles

Try to use a range of man-made and natural textiles in your designing and making. Certain man-made textiles do not take dyes at all well. Use raw cotton when you wish to dye or paint fabrics. There are several good quality dyes and dyesticks available through educational supplies companies. When purchasing fabrics it is worthwhile contacting local importing companies or garment manufacturers as you may be able to buy at good discounts or pick up scraps for little or nothing.

Textiles to buy:

- Polycotton
- Unbleached raw cotton
- Tapestry canvases
- Voiles and light polyester (decorative off-cuts)
- Felt
- Wadding.

Wood

Balsa wood This may be seen as a link between card and the softwoods. It is light and to a lesser extent flexible like card but has a natural wood grain and can be acquired in sheet, strip and block form. Balsa is relatively easy to work with, using either craft knives or saws, although if treated clumsily, has a tendency to split along the grain. You should caution children against simply snapping and breaking balsa wood instead of cutting it properly. Balsa wood can be filled, sanded and filed to produce a smooth finish or intricate shape, and can be drilled. Balsa can be stuck using PVA glue, but for preference use balsa cement. Note that this is a synthetic solvent type glue and should be used only by older children with close supervision. Because of its softness balsa can be pinned.

Hardwoods These are more dense, harder to work and are often produced at too high an environmental cost. We strongly advise you not to use them at all.

Softwoods These are harder, heavier and less flexible than balsa. They also float in water. They are available in similar forms to balsa wood and in addition are available as laminates in the form of plywood sheets. Softwoods cannot be cut with craft knives and must be cut with saws. Softwood can be stuck with PVA, resin based glues and hot glue. Small pieces of softwood will tend to split if nailed; if your pupils pre-drill smaller

holes and then screw pieces together you will find this a better method of fixing.

Tools

It is of great importance that your pupils should realise that tools have specific functions and that there will always be a preferred tool for a particular purpose. We mentioned above that your pupils should not use scissors to cut wire and this approach to the use of tools should be encouraged at all times. The selection and use of appropriate tools goes hand-in-hand with an understanding of the properties of materials and a clear definition of purpose.

At key stage 1 your pupils will be using a relatively limited range of materials and they will need a similarly limited range of tools. The materials they will most commonly use in design and technology are; balsa wood, card, clay, dough, junk, fabrics, plastic containers and plasticine.

At key stage 2, the materials that will be used include all of those for key stage 1 with the addition of the following: flexible wire, rigid metal rods, plastic sheets, rods and tubes, scrap textile materials and carpet offcuts, soft woods.

Safety

It is essential that your pupils respect and know how to use and care for tools safely and correctly. They need to be aware of the dangers of misuse. It is important that matters concerning health and safety requirements should form part of your school policy on the storage and use of tools.

Apart from tools which are inherently of poor quality, the most likely danger will occur when tools are used for an inappropriate purpose or in an inappropriate way. Additional protection from accidents can be

---

Bench hooks, vices and clamps

Cutting tools:
 Craft knives
 Drills and drill bits
 Hole punches
 Safety snips
 Saws:
  coping
  gents saw
  junior hacksaw
  padsaw
  tenon saw
  vibrating shapersaw
 Scissors
 Wire cutters

Fixing tools:
 Hammers:
  engineers
  pin/tack
 Nails and pins
 Needles
 Hot glue guns
 Pin Pushes
 Screw drivers:
  Cross-head
  Plain
 Screws

Forming tools:
 Modelling tools for clay and plasticine
 Pliers

Items in italics are particularly suitable for KS1

---

gained if your pupils wear safety glasses or goggles and protective clothing.

Dictionary of tools

Bench hooks, vices and clamps

A bench hook can provide a stable base against which to brace wood and any other materials for sawing. The end of the block on the bench hook can be used as a 'saw guide' to help make a straight cut at the desired point, or some bench hooks may have saw guides cut into the block. Other blocks have saw guides cut at specific angles of 45, 60 and/or 90 degrees. Such blocks avoid the need for you to provide additional 'mitre' blocks because mitre bench hooks will allow your pupils to make angled cuts. Bench hooks are essential items, and are reasonably inexpensive.

When using a saw with or without bench hooks and mitre blocks, there are a few simple rules that you should remember:

- The piece that is being sawn must be held securely either in a vice or a bench hook
- Keep saw blades horizontal and concentrate on keeping a smooth push and pull action along the whole length of the saw blade. Do not snatch and loose patience
- Do not try to force the blade through the material that is being cut. This will make it snag and make sawing more difficult.

The teeth on the saw blade face forward so that they cut through the wood/material on each forward stroke without needing to be forced down into the material being sawn.

Do not use bench hooks to cut into the end of pieces of wood. For such work always use a clamp or vice. Clamps can be used to add stability to the use of bench hooks, by clamping them to a table, or to hold wood on to the block of the bench hook more firmly. We recommend that vices are used for holding wood for sawing in awkward positions. Useful clamps and vices are: G- clamps, engineers' clamps, table top clamps and vices (some are available with a suction base attachment. The most expensive is the engineer type; the cheapest are G-clamps and suction base vices.

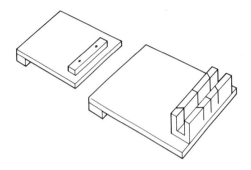

Cutting tools

Most materials (except balsa wood) at key stage 1 can be cut with scissors. For very young children blunt-nosed scissors may be safer although such scissors can cause frustration when a cut needs to be made in the middle of a piece of card or into the side of plastic bottles. Right-handed and left-handed scissors are available. For thicker plastics and card, safety snips and utility snips will be needed.

Craft knives Paper, card and sheet plastics such as polythene can still be cut with scissors or snips. As children grow they will be able to work more safely with craft knives. This tool will produce neater results than scissors and is also more appropriate for thicker or corrugated plastic sheet. Craft knives are available in several types. Some have retractable blades, some have fixed blades and are intended to be disposable, others have changeable blades or blades which snap off to give fresh points and cutting edges.

Safety is a prime consideration with all cutting tools; this is particularly important for craft knives. Always provide metal safety

rules, cutting mats and good quality sharp knives. The metal safety rule cannot be cut by knives and has a central groove to protect fingers from the blade. Always insist that fingers are kept away from the direction of the cut. Then, with the blade at a slight angle, draw the knife in a single stroke towards the body along the line of the cut.

Encourage your pupils not to employ a sawing action nor to press too hard. It is far better to establish the cut slowly and finish it by a series of several strokes. Avoid blunt blades. The greater the force needed to use a blunt tool, the lower the level of control. If your pupils lose control while forcing a craft knife they can cut themselves badly. Cutting mats are a good investment. They protect work surfaces and make the activity of cutting safer.

Drills and hole punches For making holes for screws, to accommodate dowel or metal rods, your pupils will need to use drills. There are two manual drills available: the standard hand drill and a pistol-grip drill. The pistol-grip drill is a relatively recent development that has been produced particularly for children: its mechanism is enclosed to protect young fingers. It is, however, more awkward to use and less robust than the standard hand drill. There are several drill stands for standard hand drills. These also frequently make for easier, safer use of drills.

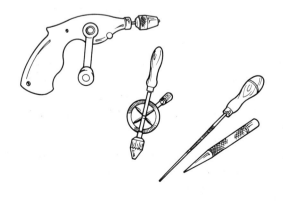

Hand drills are either single or double pinion types. These terms describe the number of gear wheels which connect the drive wheel to the drill shaft. Double pinion drills are more robust and tend to be more expensive. Loading drill bits is the same for all hand drills.

If your pupils use a drill without a drill stand make sure that they use a clamp to hold their work firmly. Make an indentation with a hammer and nail at the point where the hole is needed, then after placing the tip of the drill into the indentation, slowly turn the handle and allow the bit to do the work. When the hole has been made, continue turning the drill in the same direction and withdraw it. This makes withdrawing the drill easier and at the same time cleans the hole. Choose drill bits to match the diameter of the dowel that you use and the size of the screws most commonly used.

To make holes in softer materials such as paper and card, use a hole punch, not a drill. Single hole punches, similar to ticket punches, are limited by the distance that the hole is wanted from the edge of the material. It is better to purchase hole punches or drills that are able to be positioned anywhere on sheet material.

Saws Balsa wood and some thicker plastics should be cut with a saw. A useful basic saw is the junior hacksaw. It is light, versatile and the blades are relatively cheap and easy to replace. Sometimes because of the 'clearance' left between the blade of the junior hacksaw and the work, children find difficulty in making the final millimetre or two of any cut. For this reason it is often better to use the gents saw which is in fact a junior tenon saw.

Saws should always be used in combination with a bench hook or vice, both for your pupils' safety and to protect table surfaces.

The junior hacksaw is equally useful for cutting soft woods and metal rods as it is for balsa wood. As children become more skilled and familiar with the need for safe use of tools, other saws can be introduced. These will include:

- Tenon saw
- Padsaw
- Coping saw
- Vibrating shapersaw.

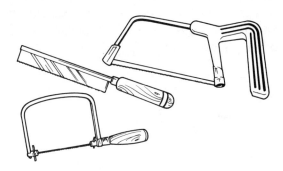

The tenon saw is a more substantial replacement for the junior hacksaw for making straight cuts. For more intricate shapes and cut-outs you will find that the padsaw and/or coping saw is most suitable. The padsaw is a frameless saw that uses hacksaw blades. As there is no frame to impede movement it is possible to make more intricate cuts. Coping saws look like hacksaws except that the blades are thinner and the frame is usually larger; the position of the blade can be altered with respect to the frame.

Vibrating shapersaws are electrically driven and, as the name suggests, operate by vibrating a thin blade at high speed. It is almost impossible to cut fingers with a shapersaw. This is because shapersaws only cut resistant materials; skin is flexible and therefore is very difficult to cut. (Fingernails *are* cut by the saw.)

It is important to emphasise to your children that not all machines are more efficient than hand tools. In the case of the shapersaw it does not cut more quickly, it merely takes away the effort required. Children may be inclined to force the saw to work more quickly. Such forcing will almost certainly result in the blades being broken. You may find such a tool to be an expensive luxury.

Utility snips These have serrated blades, and the positioning of the pivot increases leverage to apply a proportionally greater force on the cutting blades for an equivalent force on the handles. Even young children will therefore find them easier to use. Utility and safety snips are more expensive than other scissors.

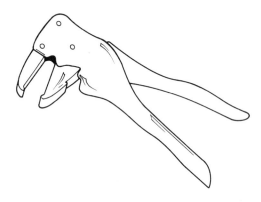

Wire cutters There are several approaches to the task of cutting and stripping wire. Wire cutters that combine cutting and stripping functions are still available. They are good sturdy tools but require fairly subtle control. When stripping wire for electrical connection, it is very easy to cut through the pvc covering and straight through the wire. An alternative is the automatic wire stripper

which is automatically adjusted and incorporates a wire cutter as well. Simple wire strippers are the cheapest tools. All the other combination tools are about the same price.

Fixing tools

For work with fabrics, needles are needed when using threads for fixing and fastening. For weaving and tapestry, blunt needles are ideal and will remove the problem of using sharp needles with very young children.

Hot glue guns This tool is becoming an increasingly common sight in schools. Children and teachers find it attractive because it has virtually universal application and is almost instant. Unchecked, this could promote indiscriminate use and a consequently high consumption of glue sticks. We do question the use of glue guns in many circumstances. Wood glues such as PVA should not be replaced without good reason. This, of course, is linked with the requirements of National Curriculum document. Also it is important for you to check your LEA policy, as some authorities do not allow the use of glue guns in primary schools. Even if you are allowed to use them you must ensure that they are used only under close supervision. Do not forget that even after the guns are switched off, the nozzle and the glue remain painfully hot for a while.

Nails and pins You will probably only need two or three basic tools such as a small pin or tack hammer for using small nails and pins. These hammers have dual shaped heads and are lightweight. An alternative is the pin driver; when loaded into the barrel, pins or nails can be pushed home by firm pressure on the spring-loaded handle.

Screws For stronger fixings, screws are preferable to nails and pins. Screws and screw drivers are of two types, plain and cross-head. Plain screw drivers tend to slip more easily than cross-headed ones such as Philips and Pozidrive. On the other hand the damaged tip of a plain screw driver can be re-sharpened while a damaged cross-headed screwdriver is useless. You will probably find that a set of three screw drivers will be sufficient for class use. These will include a small electrician's screwdriver, an engineer's screwdriver and a cross-headed Philips or Pozidrive screwdriver. Philips and Pozidrive are not identical, so ensure that you have supplies of the right kind of screws to match your screwdriver.

Forming and manipulative tools

Pliers For gripping, pulling and bending wire into different shapes, use pliers. Choose combination pliers as these incorporate a wire cutter.

Specialised wooden and plastic modelling tools These are useful for working clay and plasticine. They are available in assorted packs. Wooden tools are generally three times as expensive as plastic tools.

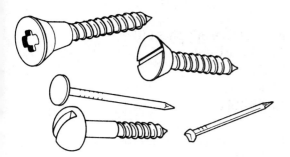

APPENDIX

Hogg Laboratory Supplies
Sloan Street
Birmingham
B1 3BW

Leisurewire Limited
309 Corporation Road
Birkenhead
Wirral
L41 1HB

Nottingham Educational Supplies
17 Ludlow Hill Road
West Bridgford
Nottingham
NG2 6HD

Proops Distributors Ltd
Unit 24D
North Tyne Industrial Estate
Whitley Road
Longbenton
Newcastle Upon Tyne
NE12 7TD

R S Components
P O Box 253
Dudderton Mill Industrial Estate
Dudderton Mill Road
Saltley
Birmingham
B8 1BQ

Solarbo Ltd
Commerce Way
Lancing
West Sussex
BN15 8TE

Spectrum Educational Supplies
Maskell Estate
Stephenson's Street
London
E16 4SA

Stanley Tools
Woodside
Sheffield
S3 9PD

Surplus Buying Agency
Woodbourn Road School
Woodbourn Road
Sheffield
S9 3LQ

Technical and Optical Equipment
Zenith House
The Hyde
Edge Road
London
NW9 6EE

Technology Teaching Systems Ltd
Penmore House
Hasland Raod
Chesterfield
S41 0SJ

Valiant Technology Limited
370 York Road
Wandsworth
London
SW18 1SP

Also available in this series

Really Practical Guides

This series is designed to provide primary teachers with up-to-date, accessible guides to good primary practice in line with the demands of the National Curriculum.

New and forthcoming titles include the following:

The Really Practical Guide to Primary Assessment	Wendy and David Clemson
The Really Practical Guide to Primary RE	Hubert Smith
The Really Practical Guide to National Curriculum 5–11	Wendy and David Clemson
The Really Practical Guide to Primary Science	Carol Holland
The Really Practical Guide to Primary Maths	Jean Livingstone and Wally Nickels
The Really Practical Guide to Primary History	Margaret Wright
The Really Practical Guide to Primary English	Pie Corbett
The Really Practical Guide to Primary Geography	Marcia Foley and Jan Janikoun

Books can be purchased over the telephone by credit card, and information obtained on (0242) 228888. Further information may also be obtained by writing to:

Marketing Services Dept
Stanley Thornes Publishers
Old Station Drive
Leckhampton
Cheltenham
Gloucestershire
GL53 0DN

The Really Practical Guide To Primary Assessment

David and Wendy Clemson

A readable and friendly guide to assessment that explains what primary school teachers, staffs and governors need to know – and how to put it into action.

- what the real issues are

- what the National Curriculum demands

- how to master the jargon of assessment

- how to make sensible choices for teacher-based assessments

- how to carry it out effectively (and stay sane!)

- how to compile practical and useful records and reports

- how to cope with the pressures of time and from parents

- how to manage assessments at school and class level

- how assessment can help you improve children's learning

A special practical workshop section provides a complete INSET package of lively and positive activities for you and your staff to use together.

What the *TES* said about this book:

> " *Refreshing ... highly readable ... the assessment requirements of the National Curriculum are clearly explained ... together with anything else a primary teacher is ever likely to want to know about assessment ... a guide to how to go about assessment and what to do with the results.* "

The Really Practical Guide To Primary History

Margaret Wright

Based on her substantial INSET work with primary schools, Margaret Wright's book is an essential aid to everyone facing National Curriculum history. It explains the document and provides clear strategies for planning and delivering National Curriculum, with particular emphasis on cross-curricular and topic approaches. There is a substantial ideas bank of activities for both key stages, advice on museums and sites, and chapters on assessment, record keeping and evaluation.

The Really Practical Guide to National curriculum 5–11

Wendy and David Clemson

A thought-provoking, readable book to help you develop your teaching further – both individually and across the whole school.

The Really Practical Guide to National Curriculum 5–11, highly praised by the *TES*, is a professional guide to better teaching and learning in primary schools.

It covers:

- the issues and how to explain them to parents
- better National Curriculum planning
- teaching through subjects and topics
- how to develop better teaching strategies
- how to manage National Curriculum more effectively
- how to tackle evaluation
- how to cope with change
- an action plan for looking at your present work and improving it – at both class and school level.

What the *TES* said about this book:

"*Clear ... concise ... original ... dynamic ... uncompromising ... down-to-earth.*"

The Really Practical Guide To Primary RE

Hubert Smith

An invaluable and up-to-date guide to planning and teaching RE in the 1990s. It explains what the law now says about teaching RE in school, what the aims of primary RE should be, how to plan an effective RE programme and how to deliver it in the classroom. Throughout, attention is given to managing RE alongside National Curriculum demands and there are special sections on assessment and resources.